Real
Listening & Speaking 1
with answers

Miles Craven

CAMBRIDGE
UNIVERSITY PRESS

CAMBRIDGE UNIVERSITY PRESS
Cambridge, New York, Melbourne, Madrid, Cape Town, Singapore, São Paulo, Delhi

Cambridge University Press
The Edinburgh Building, Cambridge CB2 8RU, UK

www.cambridge.org
Information on this title: www.cambridge.org/9780521701983

© Cambridge University Press 2008

This publication is in copyright. Subject to statutory exception
and to the provisions of relevant collective licensing agreements,
no reproduction of any part may take place without the written
permission of Cambridge University Press.

First published 2008

Printed in the United Kingdom at the University Press, Cambridge

A catalogue record for this publication is available from the British Library

ISBN-13 978-0-521-70198-3

Cambridge University Press has no responsibility for the persistence or
accuracy of URLs for external or third-party internet websites referred to in
this publication, and does not guarantee that any content on such websites is,
or will remain, accurate or appropriate.

Contents

R0415279692

CHICAGO PUBLIC LIBRARY
HEGEWISCH BRANCH
3048 E. 130TH ST.   60633

Map of the book	4
Acknowledgements	6
Introduction	7

☕ Social and Travel

Unit 1	Where are you from?	10
Unit 2	Do you need any help?	14
Unit 3	I'll have pizza, please	18
Unit 4	This is your room	22
Unit 5	One first class stamp	26
Unit 6	I don't feel very well	30
Unit 7	Your passport, please	34
Unit 8	A single room, please	38
Unit 9	When is the next train?	42
Unit 10	There's so much to see!	46
Review 1		50

Work and Study

Unit 11	I'll do it straight away	52
Unit 12	When can you deliver?	56
Unit 13	I'll put you through	60
Unit 14	Are there any questions?	64
Unit 15	What's your opinion?	68
Unit 16	I'll hand it in tomorrow	72
Review 2		76

Appendix 1	Useful language	78
Appendix 2	Pronunciation features	84
Appendix 3	Speaking strategies	85
Appendix 4	Learning tips	86
Appendix 5	Presentation evaluation	88

Audioscript	89
Answer key	101

Map of the book

Unit number	Title	Topic	How to ...
1	Where are you from?	Meeting people	○ introduce yourself in formal and informal situations ○ ask and answer questions about basic personal information ○ begin a social conversation and respond appropriately ○ greet people and say goodbye in a variety of ways
2	Do you need any help?	Shopping	○ ask an assistant for help in a shop or market ○ ask questions in a clothes shop (size, price, etc.) ○ show you understand ○ understand numbers and prices
3	I'll have pizza, please	Food and eating out	○ order a meal in a restaurant ○ ask about dishes on the menu ○ talk about food and express your opinion ○ ask about food and describe different dishes
4	This is your room	Staying with a family	○ greet people and make introductions ○ understand directions ○ understand rules ○ ask for permission ○ talk about a study abroad experience and give your opinion
5	One first class stamp	Banks, post offices, and bureaux de change	○ ask about and understand services in a bank ○ ask about services and send different types of mail in a post office ○ accept or decline services ○ change money, ask about exchange rates and commission
6	I don't feel very well	Health	○ explain common health problems ○ ask for medication and understand basic instructions at a chemist's ○ express sympathy and give advice on health problems ○ make an appointment and confirm important details
7	Your passport, please	At an airport	○ check in at an airport and go through immigration ○ provide information and give clear answers ○ ask for information about transport, facilities, etc. ○ greet friends and people you don't know
8	A single room, please	Hotels	○ ask about services and facilities in a hotel ○ check into a hotel and talk about your room ○ make a complaint in a hotel

Social and Travel

	Unit number	Title	Topic	How to ...
Social and Travel	9	When is the next train?	Travelling by train or bus	o ask about travel details o understand the time o ask for and give directions o check information to make sure you understand
	10	There's so much to see!	Tourism	o ask for information at a Tourist Information Office o make and respond to suggestions o follow a guided tour o talk about places you visit on holiday
Work and Study	11	I'll do it straight away	Helping customers and colleagues	o offer to help customers o take messages and pass messages on o understand and follow instructions o politely ask people not to do something o say goodbye to visitors
	12	When can you deliver?	Goods and services	o ask about products and services o make and respond to requests o place an order for a product o compare products and choose between alternatives
	13	I'll put you through	Phone calls	o make and receive telephone calls o take and leave messages o spell names and addresses, and say telephone numbers o leave voicemail messages
	14	Are there any questions?	Talks and presentations	o understand the organization of a presentation or talk o recognize signposts that speakers use o listen for stress on important words to help you understand o talk about a presentation
	15	What's your opinion?	Seminars and expressing opinions	o ask for clarification, and explain what you mean o agree and disagree with others o give your opinion and ask other people's opinions o interrupt someone to make a point
	16	I'll hand it in tomorrow	Class schedules	o ask about and understand schedules o understand announcements about lectures o understand instructions for homework o apologize for delays

Acknowledgements

The author would like to thank all the Cambridge University Press team involved in the development of *Real Listening & Speaking* for their commitment, enthusiasm and outstanding support; especially Nóirín Burke, Roslyn Henderson, Caroline Thiriau, Linda Matthews and Martine Walsh. Very special thanks also to Sheila Dignen, Hilary Ratcliffe and Claire Thacker for their excellent editing, and to Bell International for the use of their wonderful facilities. Finally, I would like to thank Jessica for her love, patience and support, which make all things possible.

The author and publishers are grateful to the following reviewers for their valuable insights and suggestions:

Kathryn Alevizos, UK
Steve Banfield, United Arab Emirates
Vanessa Boutefeu, Portugal
Nigel Daly, Taiwan
Rui da Silva, London
Rosie Ganne, UK
Barbara Gardner, UK
Peter Gray, Japan
Jean Greenwood, UK
Hebe Gomez, Spain
Philip Lodge, United Arab Emirates
Dr Zbigniew Mozejko, Poland
Paul Seligson, UK
Raymond Sheehan, United Arab Emirates

The publishers are grateful to the following for permission to reproduce copyright photographs and material:

Key: l = left, c = centre, r = right, t = top, b = bottom

Alamy/©Janine Wiedel Photolibrary for p. 32 /©Krzysztof Gapys for p. 38 (c) /©Ian Dagnall for p. 48 (tl) /©World Pictures for p. 48 (bl) /©Up The Resolution for p. 64; Corbis Images/©Jose Fuste Raga for p. 38 (l) /©Theo Allofs/Zefa for p. 38 (r) /©Tom Grill for p. 47 /©MedioImages for p. 54; DHL for p. 56 (c); Dinodia@LinkIndia for p. 56 (l); Getty Images/©Dorling Kindersley for p. 48 (r); Panos/©Marie Dorigny/Editing for p. 69; Photolibrary/©Tony Robins for p. 18 (t) /©PhotoDisc for p. 34; Punchstock/©Bananastock for p. 10 (tl) /©Blend Images for p. 10 (tc) /©Image 100 for p. 25 /©Somos for p. 60 /©Bananastock for p. 72; Rex for p. 48 (br), p. 56 (r); Shutterstock/©Kharidehal Abhirama Ashwin for p. 10 (tr) /©David Burrows for p. 16, /©Kevin Wang for p. 48 (tr).

Illustrations:

Kathy Baxendale pp. 28, 43b, 44, 46, 49; Mark Duffin pp. 15, 17, 18, 20, 24, 34, 42, 43t, 57, 59, 73; Stuart Holmes pp. 11, 29, 40, 52; Kamae Design pp. 23, 36, 39; Katie Mac pp. 14, 21, 30, 37; Laura Martinez pp. 12, 22, 26, 38, 55, 68; Julian Mosedale pp. 19, 35, 41, 66, 71; Valeryia Steadman pp. 10, 27, 31, 62, 74

Text design and page make-up: Kamae Design, Oxford
Cover design: Kamae Design, Oxford
Cover photo: © Getty Images
Picture research: Hilary Luckcock

Introduction

To the student

Who is *Real Listening & Speaking 1* for?

You can use this book if you are a student at elementary level and you want to improve your English listening and speaking. You can use the book alone without a teacher or you can use it in a classroom with a teacher.

How will *Real Listening & Speaking 1* help me with my listening and speaking?

Real Listening & Speaking 1 contains practical tasks to help you in everyday listening and speaking situations, e.g. at the shops, in a restaurant or travelling away from home. It also gives practice of listening and speaking in a range of work and study situations. It is designed to help you with listening and speaking tasks you will need to do when communicating in English, at home or abroad.

The exercises in each unit help you to develop useful listening skills such as listening for opinions, listening for details, and listening for the main idea. There are also lots of practical speaking strategies and tasks to help you improve your ability to communicate, and pronunciation activities too.

How is *Real Listening & Speaking 1* organized?

The book has 16 units and is divided into two sections:
- Units 1–10 – social and travel situations
- Units 11–16 – work and study situations

Every unit has:
- *Get ready to listen and speak*: introduces you to the topic of the unit
- *Learning tip*: help you improve your learning
- *Class bonus:* is an exercise you can do with other students or friends
- *Speaking strategy*: gives you useful language and strategies for communicating
- *Speak up!*: gives you practice of speaking in real situations
- *Extra practice*: gives an extra exercise for more practice
- *Can-do checklist*: helps you think about what you learnt in the unit

Most units also have:
- *Focus on*: helps you study useful grammar or vocabulary
- *Did you know?*: gives you extra information about vocabulary, different cultures, or the topic of the unit
- *Sound smart*: helps you with pronunciation

After each main section there is a review unit. The reviews help you practise the skills you learn in each section.

At the back of the book you can find:
- *Appendices*: contain lists of *Useful language* for every unit and more ideas about how to improve your listening and speaking.
- *Audioscript*: includes everything that you can hear on the audio CDs and gives information about the nationalities of the speakers.
- *Answer key*: gives correct answers and possible answers for exercises that have more than one answer.

How can I use *Real Listening & Speaking 1*?

The book is in two sections; *Social and Travel*, and *Work and Study*. The units at the end of each section of the book are more difficult than the units at the beginning of each section. However, you do not need to do the units in order. It is better to choose the units that are most interesting for you and to do them in the order you prefer.

There are many different ways you can use this book. We suggest you work in this way:
- Look in the *Contents* list and find a unit that is useful for you.
- Go to *Appendix 1* and look at the *Useful language* for the unit you want to do. You can use a dictionary to help you understand the words and expressions.
- Do the *Get ready to listen and speak* section at the start of the unit. This will introduce you to the topic of the unit.
- Do the other exercises in the unit. At the end of each exercise check your answers in the *Answer key* (only in self-study edition).
- Try to do the listening exercises without looking at the audioscript. You can read the audioscript after you finish the exercises. Some exercises ask you to respond to what you hear. You can pause the CD to give you time to say your answer.
- If your answers are wrong, study the section again to see where you made mistakes.
- If you want to do more work on this topic, do the *Extra practice* activity.
- At the end of the unit, think about what you learnt and complete the *Can do checklist*.
- Go to *Appendix 1* and look at the *Useful Language* for the unit again.

Introduction
To the teacher

What is *Cambridge English Skills*?

Real Listening & Speaking 1 is one of 12 books in the *Cambridge English Skills* series. The series also contains *Real Reading* and *Real Writing* books and offers skills training to students from elementary to advanced level. All the books are available in with-answers and without-answers editions.

Level	Book	Author
Elementary CEF: A2 Cambridge ESOL: KET NQF Skills for life: Entry 2	Real Reading 1 with answers	Liz Driscoll
	Real Reading 1 without answers	Liz Driscoll
	Real Writing 1 with answers and audio CD	Graham Palmer
	Real Writing 1 without answers	Graham Palmer
	Real Listening & Speaking 1 with answers and audio CDs (2)	Miles Craven
	Real Listening & Speaking 1 without answers	Miles Craven
Pre-intermediate CEF: B1 Cambridge ESOL: PET NQF Skills for life: Entry 3	Real Reading 2 with answers	Liz Driscoll
	Real Reading 2 without answers	Liz Driscoll
	Real Writing 2 with answers and audio CD	Graham Palmer
	Real Writing 2 without answers	Graham Palmer
	Real Listening & Speaking 2 with answers and audio CDs (2)	Sally Logan & Craig Thaine
	Real Listening & Speaking 2 without answers	Sally Logan & Craig Thaine
Intermediate to upper-intermediate CEF: B2 Cambridge ESOL: FCE NQF Skills for life: Level 1	Real Reading 3 with answers	Liz Driscoll
	Real Reading 3 without answers	Liz Driscoll
	Real Writing 3 with answers and audio CD	Roger Gower
	Real Writing 3 without answers	Roger Gower
	Real Listening & Speaking 3 with answers and audio CDs (2)	Miles Craven
	Real Listening & Speaking 3 without answers	Miles Craven
Advanced CEF: C1 Cambridge ESOL: CAE NQF Skills for life: Level 2	Real Reading 4 with answers	Liz Driscoll
	Real Reading 4 without answers	Liz Driscoll
	Real Writing 4 with answers and audio CD	Simon Haines
	Real Writing 4 without answers	Simon Haines
	Real Listening & Speaking 4 with answers and audio CDs (2)	Miles Craven
	Real Listening & Speaking 4 without answers	Miles Craven

Where are the teacher's notes?

The series is accompanied by a dedicated website containing detailed teaching notes and extension ideas for every unit of every book. Please visit www.cambridge.org/englishskills to access the *Cambridge English Skills* teacher's notes.

What are the main aims of *Real Listening & Speaking 1*?

- To encourage autonomous learning by focusing on learner training.
- To help students develop listening and speaking skills in accordance with the ALTE (Association of Language Testers in Europe) Can-do statements. These statements describe what language users can typically do at different levels and in different contexts. Visit www.alte.org for further information.

What are the key features of *Real Listening & Speaking 1*?

- It is aimed at elementary learners of English at level A2 of the Council of Europe's CEFR (Common European Framework of Reference for Languages).
- It contains 16 four-page units, divided into two sections: Social and Travel, and Work and Study.
- *Real Listening and Speaking 1* units contain:
  - *Get ready to listen and speak* warm-up tasks to get students thinking about the topic
  - *Learning tip* boxes which give students advice on how to improve their listening and speaking, and their learning
  - *Focus on* activities which provide contextualized
  - *Sound smart* activities which focus on pronunciation practice in particular language or vocabulary areas
  - *Class bonus* communication activities for pairwork and group work so you can adapt the material to suit your classes
  - *Did you know?* boxes which provide notes on cultural or linguistic differences between English-speaking countries, or factual information on the topic of the unit
  - *Can-do checklists* at the end of every unit to encourage students to think about what they have learnt
- It covers a wide range of highly practical activities that give students the skills they need to communicate effectively in everyday situations.
- There are two review units to practise skills that have been introduced in the units.
- It has an international feel and contains a range of native and non-native English accents.
- It can be used as self-study material, in class, or as supplementary homework material.

What is the best way to use *Real Listening & Speaking 1* in the classroom?

The book is designed so that there is no set way to work through the units. The units may be used in any order, although the more difficult units naturally appear near the end of the book, in the *Work and Study* section.

You can consult the unit-by-unit teachers' notes at www.cambridge.org/englishskills for detailed teaching ideas. However, as a general guide, different parts of the book can be approached in the following ways:

- *Useful language*: Use the *Useful language* lists in the *Appendices* to preteach or revise the vocabulary from the unit you are working on.
- *Get ready to listen and speak*: It is a good idea to use this section as an introduction to the topic. Students can work on these exercises in pairs or groups. Many of the exercises require students to answer questions about their personal experience. These questions can be used as prompts for discussion. Some exercises contain a problem-solving element that students can work on together. Other exercises aim to clarify key vocabulary in the unit. You can present these vocabulary items directly to students.
- *Learning tips*: Focus on these and draw attention to them in an open class situation. An alternative approach is for you to create a series of discussion questions associated with the *Learning tip*. Students can discuss their ideas in pairs or small groups followed by open class feedback. The *Learning tip* acts as a reflective learning tool to help promote learner autonomy.
- *Class bonuses*: The material in these activities aims to provide freer practice. You can set these up carefully, then take the role of observer during the activity so that students carry out the task freely. You can make yourself available to help students or analyze the language they produce during the activity.
- *Extra practice*: These can be set as homework or out-of-class projects for your students. Students can do some tasks in pairs during class time.
- *Can-do checklists*: Refer to these at the beginning of a lesson to explain to students what the lesson will cover, and again at the end so that students can evaluate their learning for themselves.
- *Appendices*: You may find it useful to refer your students to these.
- *Audioscripts*: Occasionally non-native speaker spoken errors are included in the audio material. They are labelled *Did you notice?* in the audioscript and can be used in the classroom to focus on common errors.

Unit 1
Where are you from?

go to Useful language p. 78

Get ready to listen and speak

● When you meet someone you don't know, do you prefer to talk or to listen?
  Tick ✓ the adjectives that describe you.

sociable ☐   friendly ☐   shy ☐
talkative ☐   polite ☐   easy-going ☐

A Listening – Introducing yourself

1 🔊12 Listen to conversations a and b. Write a or b next to the correct picture (1 or 2).

2 🔊12 Listen again and complete the sentences.

_____I'm_____ Jake.
_____ Samantha.
_____ Vladimir Petrov.
_____ Yoko Shirai.

3 Which conversation (a or b) is more formal? _____

1 ☐   2 ☐

4 🔊12 Now listen to conversations c–g. Tick ✓ Formal or Informal.

	Formal	Informal
c	☐	✓
d	☐	☐
e	☐	☐
f	☐	☐
g	☐	☐

Did you know ...?

In the UK, people often shake hands when they first meet. In Japan, people give a bow. In France, they sometimes kiss on each cheek. How do people in your country greet each other when they first meet?

B Listening – Exchanging personal information

🔊 3 Listen to Daniela, Joshua and Shizuka talk about themselves. Complete the chart.

	is from …	is a …	lives in …
Daniela	Italy	....	....
Joshua	....	....	....
Shizuka	....	....	....

Focus on …
saying hello

ab C def

1 Complete the conversations using the words below.

   How   well   things   bad   Fine   going

   a A: Hello. How's it __going__ ?
      B: Oh, not too _____ , thanks.
   b A: Hi there. How are _____ ?
      B: _____ , thanks.
   c A: Good morning. _____ are you?
      B: I'm very _____ , thank you. And you?

2 Which conversation is formal; a, b or c? _____

Sound smart
Intonation to show interest

1 🔊 4 Listen to sentence **a** twice. Notice how the second speaker moves her voice up and down to sound more interested.

   a So you work with computers?

2 🔊 4 Listen to sentences b–g. Tick (✓) which speaker sounds more interested, Speaker 1 or Speaker 2.

	1	2
b	☐	✓
c	☐	☐
d	☐	☐
e	☐	☐
f	☐	☐
g	☐	☐

3 🔊 4 Now listen and repeat. Try to make your voice move up and down to sound interested.

C Speaking – Taking the initiative

Speaking strategy: Starting a conversation

1 **Read the conversation starters (a–d) and match them to the situations (1–4)**

   a Terrible weather today, isn't it?
   b Excuse me. Is anyone sitting here?
   c I'm looking forward to the weekend.
   d Hi. Great music, isn't it?

   1 on a train
   2 at a party
   3 at work
   4 at a bus stop

Speak up!

2 **Imagine you are in these situations. Look at each picture and start a conversation. Speak your answers.**

   Example: a
   You say: Hi. Great music, isn't it?

D Listening – Making small talk

1 🔊 **5 Listen to Ang and Teresa have a conversation. Tick ✓ the topics they talk about.**

work ☐
family ☐
home town ☐
sport ☐
hobbies ☐
holidays ☐
weather ☑
gardening ☐

2 🔊 **6 Listen and complete these questions.**

a Where are you ....from......... ?
b What do you .... ?
c Are you .... ?
d Do you have any .... ?
e Do you enjoy your .... ?
f Do you have any plans for the .... ?

3 🔊 **6 Listen again. Pause the recording after each question and answer with information about yourself.**

Example:
You hear: a
　　　　Where are you from?
You say:　I'm from Paris.

4 Look at these parts of conversations.

A: Do you play golf?
B Yes. I love golf. How about you?

A: Where are you from?
B: I'm from Madrid. What about you?

Ⓒircle the correct answer.

We use **How about you** and **What about you** to *ask the same question / ask a different question.*

5 🔊 **6 Listen again. Pause the recording after each question. Answer the questions, then ask** *What about you?* **or** *How about you?*

Example:
You hear: a
　　　　Where are you from?
You say:　I'm from Paris. How about you?

Learning tip

Remember to smile, and keep good eye contact when you are speaking to someone. This shows you are interested.

E Speaking – Reacting to what you hear

Speaking strategy: Responding to information

1 ●⑤ **Look at the expressions you can use to respond with interest. Listen again to the conversation between Teresa and Ang and tick ✓ the expressions you hear.**

Oh yes.   Oh, really?   That's interesting.
I didn't know that.   That's good.
How amazing!

Speak up!

2 ●⑦ **Listen to each statement and respond using one of the expressions above. If possible, ask a question, too.**

Example:
You hear: a
              I'm from Manchester.
You say: Really? What's it like?

Focus on ...
saying goodbye

1 Complete the conversations using the words below.

See   Good   now   Bye

a A: Bye for .... now ....
   B: OK. Bye. .... you later.
b A: .... night. It was lovely to see you.
   B: Thanks for coming. I hope you have a safe journey.
c A: .... , then. Have a good day.
   B: Thanks, bye.

2 Which conversation is formal; a, b or c? ....

Class bonus – class role play

Imagine you are at a party. Stand up and mingle with your classmates. Introduce yourself and make small talk. Try to sound interested and keep each conversation going by asking questions.

E☒tra practice

Look in the local newspaper or on the Internet to find a social event where people will speak English (for example, an event at the British Council, or a party at a language school). Take a friend and have fun!

Can-do checklist

Tick what you can do.

	Can do	Need more practice
I can introduce myself in formal and informal situations.		
I can ask and answer questions about basic personal information.		
I can begin a social conversation and respond appropriately.		
I can greet people and say goodbye in a variety of ways.		

Unit 2
Do you need any help?

go to Useful language p. 79

Get ready to listen and speak

- Do you like going shopping for clothes?
  ☺ Yes. I love it!   ☺ It's OK.   ☹ No, I hate it!

- Where do you usually buy your clothes?
  designer stores ☐
  markets ☐
  department stores ☐
  catalogues ☐
  the Internet ☐

- Look at the picture and identify each item of clothing.
  a hat _b_   jeans _____   a jacket _____   a shirt _____
  shoes _____   shorts _____   a suit _____   a sweater _____
  trousers _____

A Listening – In a clothes shop

1 🔊 **B** **Carlos is from Spain. He is visiting London, and goes shopping. Listen to the conversation and tick ✓ the items he buys.**

a shirt ☐   a pair of shorts ☐   a suit ☐
a jacket ☐   a pair of jeans ☐

2 🔊 **B** **Listen again and answer the questions.**

a When does the sale finish? _today_
b How much does the shirt cost? _____
c Is the jacket in the sale? _____
d What is the jacket made of? _____
e Where is the jacket from? _____
f Does Carlos try on the shirt? _____
g What size is the shirt? _____
h How much does Carlos spend? _____

Learning tip

Before you listen, always read the questions and make sure you know what information you are listening for (e.g. a date, a name, a price, etc.).

3 🔊 **B** **Now listen again and complete these expressions.**

a Do you need any _help_ ?
b I'm just _____ .
c How _____ is it?
d Would you like to _____ it on?
e Ok then. I'll _____ it.

4 **Look at the expressions in exercise 3. Who do you think is speaking? Write C (customer) or S (shop assistant) for each expression (a–e) above.**

a _S_   b _____   c _____
d _____   e _____

Focus on ...
singular and plural

Complete the sentences using *is* or *are*.
a How much _is_ this sweater, please?
b How much _____ these jeans?
c _____ this hat in the sale?
d Excuse me. Where _____ the changing rooms?
e I like these trousers. _____ they in the sale?
f How much _____ the black shoes over there?
g What size _____ this jacket?
h Where _____ the cash desk, please?

B Speaking – At the shops

Speaking strategy: Showing you understand

1 Read this part of Carlos's conversation. <u>Underline</u> the expressions Carlos uses to show he understands.

Assistant: That shirt's in the sale. Today's the last day.
Carlos: Oh, right. Hmm. Well, I like the colour.
Assistant   It's £20 in the sale. The normal price is forty.
Carlos: Oh, OK. That's quite good.

Speak up!

2 Match the sentences (a–e) with the replies (1–5).

a Yes, we've got this T-shirt in your size.
b The changing rooms are over there.
c I'm sorry. We haven't got this in small.
d These jeans are in the sale.
e I'm afraid we don't accept cheques.

1 OK. I'll go and try this on.
2 Oh, right. What size are they?
3 Oh, right. I'll pay by credit card.
4 Oh, OK. I'll leave it.
5 OK. I'll take it.

3 Look at the replies. Which expression means:

a I'll buy it. _____
b I won't buy it. _____

4 🎵9 Imagine you are a customer in a clothes shop. Listen to the shop assistant and reply. Use an expression to show you understand, and say if you want to buy the item or not.

Example:
You hear: a
          No, I'm sorry. We haven't got this T-shirt in medium.
You say: Oh, OK. I'll leave it, then.

Sound smart
Sentence stress

In English, the important words in a sentence have more stress. This means we say them louder.

1 🎵10 Listen to sentences a–d. Notice how the <u>underlined</u> words have more stress.
   a Do you <u>need</u> any <u>help</u>?
   b That <u>jacket's</u> in the <u>sale</u>.
   c What <u>size</u> do you <u>want</u>?
   d <u>Thank</u> you, I'll <u>take</u> it.

2 🎵10 Listen to questions e–j and underline the important words that have more stress.
   e How much is this hat?
   f Are these shoes in the sale?
   g Where's the cash desk?
   h Can I pay by cheque?
   i Do you have this shirt in medium?
   j Where are the changing rooms, please?

3 🎵10 Listen again and repeat each question, adding stress to the important words.

a

b

c

d

e

f

C Listening – At a market

🎧11 **Kumiko is from Japan. She is shopping at a market in London. Listen and write true (T) or false (F) for each statement.**

a Kumiko wants to buy a coat. T

b It costs £130. ......

c It's made of leather. ......

d It's from France. ......

e She thinks it's a bargain. ......

f The man says it's half price. ......

g She decides to buy it for £100. ......

h She pays by credit card. ......

Did you know ...?

There are lots of informal words for money. In Britain people often use *quid* instead of *pounds*: *This bag cost twenty quid.* (Notice that *quid* is never plural.) In Britain, a *fiver* is a £5 note, and in the US a dollar is often called a *buck*.

D Listening – Understanding numbers; prices

1 Before you listen, match each price (a–f) with a price tag (1–6).

a ten dollars and fifty cents 4

b one ninety-nine ......

c five euros and fifty cents ......

d four dollars fifty ......

e three fifty ......

f two pounds and ninety-nine pence ......

1 ○ £3.50

2 ○ £2.99

3 ○ $4.50

4 ○ $10.50

5 ○ €5.50

6 ○ £1.99

2 🎧12 Listen to a–f and (circle) the prices that you hear.

a (£13) / £30

b $14 / $40

c €15 / €50

d £16 / £60

e €17 / €70

f $18 / $80

3 🎧13 Listen to a–f and write down the prices of these clothes.

a T-shirt .... £3.99 ....

b jeans ....

c jacket ....

d shirt ....

e shoes ....

f jumper ....

E Speaking – In a clothes shop

Speaking strategy: Asking a shop assistant for help

1 You can use these expressions to ask a shop assistant for help. Write the words in the correct order.

a help / me. / you / Can / me, / Excuse / please?
  Excuse me. Can you help me, please?

b me. / help / please? / Could / Excuse / you / me,
  ....

c think / help / you / Do / you / could / me?
  ....

Speak up!

2 (●14) Number each line of the conversation in order (1–6). Then listen and check.

...... Oh, OK. Can I try them on?
..1... Excuse me. Can you help me, please?
...... Er, let me have a look. Here it is. They're £35.
...... Yes, of course. How can I help?
...... How much are these trousers? I can't find the price.
...... Yes, of course. The changing rooms are over there.

3 (●14) Listen again. Pause the recording and repeat the customer's words.

4 Imagine you are a customer in a clothes shop. Use the ideas below and ask a shop assistant for help.

Example: a
You say: Excuse me. Can you help me, please?
        How much are these shoes?

a

price?

b

size?

c

medium?

d

where?

e   in the sale?

Class bonus

Half the class are shop assistants, the other half are customers.

Customers: Work individually. Make a shopping list of five items of clothing you want to buy. Then go shopping! Talk to different shop assistants and tell them what you want to buy. Do they have the size you want? Ask about the price. Try to buy all the items on your list.

Shop assistants: Work individually. Make a list of five items of clothing in your shop and add the prices. Are any items in the sale? Then talk to different customers. Try to sell as much as you can.

E X tra practice

Go to the BBC *Learning English* website and type 'going shopping listen' in the search box. Press enter, then click on a link that interests you. Find something to watch or listen to, and complete any exercises.
http://www.bbc.co.uk/worldservice/learningenglish

Can-do checklist

Tick what you can do.

	Can do	Need more practice
I can ask an assistant for help in a shop or market.		
I can ask questions in a clothes shop about size, price, etc.		
I can show I can understand.		
I can understand numbers and prices.		

Unit3
I'll have pizza, please

go to Useful language p. 79

Get ready to listen and speak

- How often do you eat out?
- What kind of restaurants do you like to go to?
  expensive restaurants ☐
  small, local restaurants ☐
  family restaurants ☐
  fast food restaurants ☐

A Listening – Ordering a meal in a restaurant

1 🔊**15** **Listen to these sentences. Who do you think is speaking? Tick ✓ Customer or Waiter.**

	Customer	Waiter
a	☐	✓
b	☐	☐
c	☐	☐
d	☐	☐
e	☐	☐
f	☐	☐
g	☐	☐
h	☐	☐
i	☐	☐

2 🔊**16** **Imagine you are a customer in a restaurant. Listen to the waiter's questions. Match each question (a–e) with a reply (1–5).**

a   1 French onion soup, please.
b   2 No, thanks. I'm full. I'll just have a coffee, please.
c   3 I'll have steak, please.
d   4 I'll have a glass of mineral water, thank you.
e   5 Yes, I am. Thank you.

3 🔊**16** **Listen again. Pause the recording after each question and say the correct reply.**

4 🔊**16** **Listen to the questions once more. Use the ideas below to reply.**

Example:
You hear: a
     Can I get you anything to drink?
You say: I'll have a glass of orange juice, please.

Did you know …?

British English and American English are sometimes different.

American English		British English
appetizer	=	starter
entrée	=	main course
check	=	bill

B Speaking – Understanding the menu

Speaking strategy: Asking about dishes on a menu

1 You can use the expressions in **bold** to ask someone to explain something on the menu.

Excuse me. **What's a** Caesar Salad?
What's in the Mexican Mixed Grill?
Can you tell me what the House Special **is**, please?

Speak up!

2 Look at the menu and imagine you are in a restaurant. You want the waiter to explain what these dishes are. What can you say? Speak your answers.

Example: a
You say: Excuse me. What's a Waldorf Salad?

Excuse me. What's Death by Chocolate, please?

Menu

Starters

Vegetable Soup
ªWaldorf Salad

Main course

Steak
ᵇSpaghetti Carbonara
ᶜMexican Chicken

Desserts

Fruit Salad
ᵈSummer Fruits Pudding

Learning tip

If possible, prepare yourself *before* you listen or speak in English. Think of the language that you might hear, and what you might need to say.

Sound smart
Intonation in questions

1 🔊17 Listen to questions a–f and notice the intonation.

a Do you want dessert?   b Can I take your coat?

c Where do you want to sit?

d What would you like as a starter?

2 Circle the correct answer to complete the rule.
For questions that have a *Yes/No* answer, your voice usually goes a) … UP/DOWN … at the end of the sentence. For questions that begin *Wh-*, your voice usually goes b) … UP/DOWN … at the end of the sentence.

3 🔊18 Look at questions a–h. Decide if the intonation goes up or down at the end. Tick ✓ your answers, then listen and check.

		↗	↘
a	Could I have a menu, please?	......	✓
b	What do you recommend?	......	......
c	Do you have a set menu?	......	......
d	What soft drinks do you have?	......	......
e	Can I have the bill, please?	......	......
f	Is service included?	......	......
g	What specials do you have today?	......	......
h	Where's the toilet, please?	......	......

4 Now listen and repeat each question, using the correct intonation.

C Listening – Talking about food

1 🔊 **19** Listen to four people talk about their food in a restaurant. Look at the menu. Which dish is each person describing?

a Beef and vegetables ....

b ....

c ....

d ....

2 🔊 **19** Listen again. What adjectives does each person use to describe their food?

a excellent, tender, tasty ....

b ....

c ....

d ....

Bistro **42**

Lunch menu

Tomato soup
Green salad
....
Chicken curry with rice
Fish and chips
Beef and vegetables
....
Fruit salad
Apple pie and ice-cream

€19

Focus on ...
words describing food

ab**c**def

1 Circle the adjective that does *not* describe each of these types of food.

a salad: fresh, crunchy, rich
b chicken: tender, spicy, soft, tasty
c ice-cream: sweet, salty, creamy
d sauce: mild, rich, tough

2 Look at these words and expressions you can use to describe food. Write each one in the correct column.

> all right, awful, delicious, excellent, not very good, OK, really tasty

☺	☺	☹
....	....	....
....	....	....
....		

D Speaking – Giving opinions about food

Speaking strategy: Asking for and expressing opinions

1 You can use the expressions in **bold** to ask someone about their food.

What's the soup **like**? **How's your** salad? **Is** the steak **nice**?

Speak up!

2 Imagine you are with some friends in a restaurant. Look at what your friends are eating. Ask them about their food.

Example: a
You say: What's your burger like?

a burger
b steak
c chicken
d salad
e spaghetti

3 🔊 **20** Imagine you are eating these dishes. Listen to the questions from your friend, then use the ideas below to reply. Use the adjectives in Focus on ... to help you.

Example:
You hear: a
    What's your soup like?
You say: It's very tasty.

a ☺   b ☺
c ☹   d ☺
e ☺

E Listening – Fast food

In a fast food restaurant, people speak quite quickly, and often they do not use full sentences.

1 🔵 **21** Listen to this conversation and complete the customer's order.

.... cheeseburger
.... fries
a small ....

2 🔵 **21** Listen again. How much does the meal cost? $ ....

PRICES
SMALL COFFEE $1.00
REGULAR COFFEE $1.50
LARGE COFFEE $2.00

Class bonus

Work in groups of three or four. Choose one person to be the waiter. Use the Bistro 42 menu.

Waiter: Take each person's order. Explain the dishes on the menu where necessary. Then serve your customers!

Customers: Decide what to order. Ask the waiter to explain any dishes you don't know. During the meal describe each dish.

Learning tip

In a fast food restaurant, look at the pictures around you and the words on the menu board like *large, regular* and *small*.

E X tra practice

Watch a cooking programme in English on satellite or cable TV, or listen to a programme about food on the radio in English. Perhaps you can find a good recipe to try out at home!

Can-do checklist

Tick what you can do.

	Can do	Need more practice
I can order a meal in a restaurant.		
I can ask about dishes on a menu.		
I can talk about food and express my opinion.		
I can ask about food and describe different dishes.		
I can say that I don't understand.		

Unit 4
This is your room

go to Useful language p. 79

Get ready to listen and speak

- When you are studying abroad, do you think it is better to stay with a family or live with other students?

- What are the benefits of each experience? Tick ✓ your answers.

	living with a family	living with other students	both
You can learn about the lifestyle and culture.	☐	☐	☐
You can practise your English.	☐	☐	☐
You can make friends easily.	☐	☐	☐
You can try the local food.	☐	☐	☐
It's relaxing and comfortable.	☐	☐	☐
You can get help with your homework.	☐	☐	☐

- Which of these benefits are most important to you?

A Speaking – Greetings and introductions

Speaking strategy: Meeting people for the first time

1 Paula is a student from Brazil. She is staying with a family in Ireland. Read the conversation and notice the expressions in **bold**.

Mrs Woods: Paula, **I'd like you to meet** my husband.
Paula: **Nice to meet you**, Mr Woods.
Mr Woods: **Nice to meet you too**, Paula. Please **call me** Kevin.
Mrs Woods: And **this is** my daughter, Abigail.
Paula: Hello, Abigail. **Pleased to meet you.**
Abigail: Hi. How was your trip?
Paula: It was fine, thanks.

2 Write the expressions you can use:

a to introduce someone (2 expressions)
  I'd like you to meet ....
b when you meet someone for the first time (2 expressions)
  ....
c to reply when someone says, 'Nice to meet you' ....
d to tell someone your preferred name ....

Speak up!

3 🔊 122 Imagine you are staying with a family in England. You are meeting the family for the first time. Listen to the conversation and reply using the expressions above.

Example:
You hear: ...
    Now, I'd like you to meet my wife, Carol.
    Hello. Nice to meet you.
You say: a
    Nice to meet you, too.

B Listening – Understanding directions

1 **Match each expression (a–g) with a picture (1–7).**

a on the left __4__
b on the right _____
c at the top of _____
d at the bottom of _____
e at the end of _____
f next to _____
g opposite _____

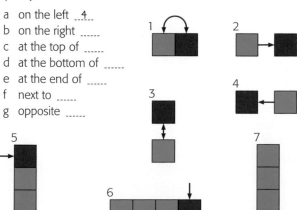

2 **📀 23 Mrs Woods is showing Paula around the house. Listen and write the letter (a–h) of each room in the correct place on the plan.**

a bathroom   d Mr/Mrs Woods' room   g Paula's room
b toilet   e Abigail's room   h dining room
c lounge   f kitchen

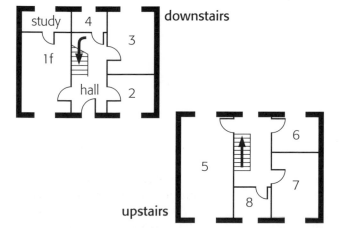

3 **📀 24 Now listen to these sentences. Write true (T) or false (F) for each sentence.**

a __T__   b _____   c _____   d _____   e _____   f _____
g _____   h _____

Did you know ...?

In the UK public toilets are often called the *Ladies* and *Gents*. You may also hear someone ask *Where's the loo?* In American English people say *restroom* or *bathroom*.

Sound smart
Linking words together

1 We often link words together when we speak.
   📀 25 Listen to sentences a and b and notice how the words are linked.

   a This is the dining room and on the right is the lounge.
   b The kitchen is on the left.

2 📀 25 Read sentences c–g. Underline the sounds that you think are linked. Then listen and check.
   c My room is on the right.
   d It's a big room with a view of the park.
   e Teresa picked up the bag and took it upstairs.
   f We left our coats in the kitchen.
   g I'd like a cup of tea, please.

3 📀 25 Listen again and repeat each sentence. Practise linking the sounds.

Focus on ...
modal verbs

1 Read these sentences and match each modal verb in **bold** (a–d) with a meaning (1–4).
   a I **can** watch TV in my room. __3__
   b I **have to** get up early every morning. _____
   c I **can't** smoke anywhere in the building. _____
   d I **don't have to** study at weekends. _____

   1 It's necessary.   2 It's not necessary.
   3 It's possible.   4 It's not possible.

2 Complete these sentences using a modal verb from above.
   a I have my own TV so I ___can___ watch what I want.
   b I _____ travel far to get to school. It's very close.
   c We all _____ keep the kitchen and bathroom clean.
   d We _____ play loud music at night, or have any pets.
   e We _____ go out in the evening, but we _____ be back before midnight.
   f I _____ cook. Meals are included in the price.

C Listening – Understanding rules

1 26 **Listen to Mrs Woods explain some rules to Paula. Number each topic she mentions in order (1–6).**

...... house key
...... washing clothes
...... using the phone
...... bathroom
..1.. meal times
...... Paula's room

Learning tip

In English, people say *please* and *thank you* a lot. Always use *please* and *thank you* whenever possible when you are speaking in English.

2 26 **Listen again and tick ✓ True or False for each rule.**

		True	False
a	You don't have to be on time for breakfast.	✓	☐
b	In the morning, you can't use the bathroom until seven o'clock.	☐	☐
c	You don't have to wash your towels and sheets.	☐	☐
d	You can do your washing on Saturdays.	☐	☐
e	You can't use the phone to call anyone.	☐	☐
f	You have to come back home before 12pm.	☐	☐

D Speaking – Asking for permission

Speaking strategy: Asking for permission

1 You can use the expressions in bold to ask for permission.

Is it OK if I watch TV?
Do you think I could make a cup of coffee?
Would you mind if I invite a friend for dinner?

Speak up!

2 Use the table below to make sentences asking for permission.

Example: Do you think I could make a cup of tea?

	turn up	a bath?
Is it OK if I …	go out	the washing machine?
Do you think I could …	have	the heating?
Would you mind if I …	use	with some friends tonight?
	make	a cup of tea?

3 Imagine you are staying with a family. You want to do these things. Ask for permission politely.

Example: a
You say: Is it OK if I use the washing machine?

a   b   c   d   e

VERY LOW

E Speaking – Talking about your experience

Speaking strategy: Expressing opinions

1 **You can use these words and expressions to give your opinion. Write each word or expression in the correct column.**

| quite good | great | fantastic | terrible | very friendly |
| really helpful | OK | not very kind | good fun | a bit boring |

a ☺	b ☺	c ☹
good fun		

Speak up!

2 **Imagine you are studying English in Australia, and are staying with a family. You are telling a friend about your experience. Use the ideas below, and use the expressions above to help you.**

Example: a
You say: The food at the school is terrible!

a ☹ the food at the school
b ☺ meals with the family
c ☺ the family
d ☺ the weather
e ☺ the school/classes

E X tra practice

Think of an English-speaking country you would like to visit, and find out about studying there. Make a list of questions you want to ask, and phone the Embassy. Ask to talk to someone from the country who can answer your questions. There may also be lectures you can go to giving more information.

Class bonus

1 Imagine you went on a study abroad holiday last year. Make notes.
   a Where did you go?
   b Where did you stay? (e.g. with a family, with other students)
   c Describe the place you stayed. (e.g. How big was it? / Where was your room?)
   d What rules were there?
   e Did you enjoy your experience? (e.g. food, weather, classes, etc.)
2 Now tell your classmates.

Can-do checklist

Tick what you can do.

	Can do	Need more practice
I can greet people and make introductions.		
I can understand rules.		
I can ask for permission.		
I can talk about a study abroad experience and give my opinion.		
I can understand directions.		

One first class stamp

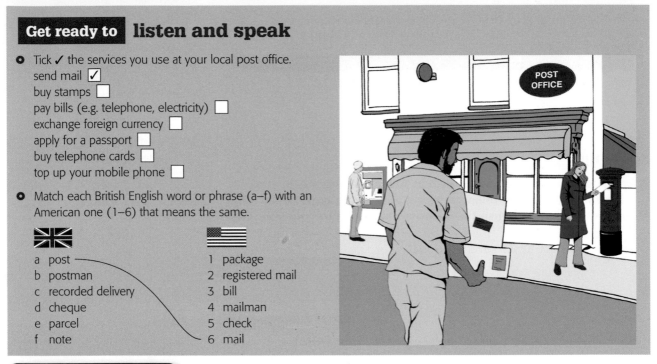

Get ready to listen and speak

- Tick ✓ the services you use at your local post office.
  - send mail ✓
  - buy stamps ☐
  - pay bills (e.g. telephone, electricity) ☐
  - exchange foreign currency ☐
  - apply for a passport ☐
  - buy telephone cards ☐
  - top up your mobile phone ☐

- Match each British English word or phrase (a–f) with an American one (1–6) that means the same.

a post	1 package
b postman	2 registered mail
c recorded delivery	3 bill
d cheque	4 mailman
e parcel	5 check
f note	6 mail

go to Useful language p. 80

A Listening – Asking about services

1 🔊 **27** **Listen to these customers. Tick ✓ where you think each person is.**

	In a bank	In a post office
a	☐	✓
b	☐	☐
c	☐	☐
d	☐	☐
e	☐	☐
f	☐	☐
g	☐	☐

Learning tip

Listen for key words to help you identify each place. For example, if you hear *stamps*, then it must be a post office!

2 🔊 **27** **Listen again. What does each person want to do?**

- a buy ten *first class stamps* ....
- b open a ....
- c send a .... to ....
- d order a new ....
- e check his ....
- f send a .... by ....
- g send a letter by .... delivery

3 🔊 **27** **Listen again and repeat each sentence.**

Did you know …?

In the USA, people say an *ATM*, but in the UK it is usually called a *cash machine* or *cashpoint*. It is also called a *Bancomat* in Italy, Switzerland and many other European countries, and an *ABM* in Canada! What is it called in your country?

B Listening – In a bank

1 **♦28** Listen to a bank clerk explain how to open a new account. What documents do you need? Complete the notes.

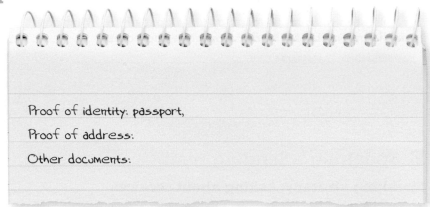

Proof of identity: passport,

Proof of address:

Other documents:

2 **♦29** Listen to the bank clerk. Tick ✓ the things you can do with this bank account.

take out money ☑
borrow money ☐
pay in cash/cheques ☐
have a credit card ☐
use a cheque book ☐
have a cash card ☐

3 **♦30** Listen to three short conversations in a bank. What service does each person want?

a open a bank account
b ....
c ....

4 **♦30** Listen again. What does the bank clerk ask each person to do?

a fill in a form
b ....
c ....

Focus on ...
money

1 Look at the phrases below. Can you complete the missing verbs?

a op_en_____ a bank account.
b se_____ a parcel
c or_____ a new cheque book
d ca_____ a cheque
e ex_____ foreign currency
f ch_____ your balance

2 Match each word (a–e) with a definition (1–5).

a transfer (v)   1 the amount of money you have in your account
b withdraw (v)   2 money you borrow from a bank
c deposit (v)   3 to take money out from an account
d loan (n)   4 to pay money into an account
e balance (n)   5 to move money from one account to another

C Speaking – Using a bank account

Speaking strategy: Explaining what you want

1 **♦30** You can use these expressions to explain what you want. Listen again and write the customer (a–c) next to the expression that they use.

I'd like to ...... I need to ...... I want to ......

Speak up!

2 Put the words in order to complete each sentence.

a £200 / want / pay / account / my / into / I / to
   I want to pay £200 into my account.
b withdraw / to / like / $400 / I'd
   ....
c have to / money / abroad / send / some / I
   ....
d account / open / like / to / I'd / an
   ....

3 Imagine you are in a bank. Use the ideas below to make sentences explaining what you want.

Example: a
You say: I'd like to pay £100 into my account, please.

a  b

c

d £1000 → bank account in Mexico
e new account

D Listening – In a post office

1 🔊31 Listen to four conversations in a post office. What does each customer want to do? Complete the notes.

a send three __postcards__ to _____ by _____ .
b send a _____ to _____ by _____ .
c send a _____ to _____ .
d send a _____ to _____ by _____ .

2 🔊31 Listen again. How much does each person pay?

a __£1.50__ _____
b _____
c _____
d _____

E Speaking – Sending mail

Speaking strategy: Asking about services

1 🔊31 Listen to the conversations again. Tick ✓ the expressions you hear.

Can I send this letter by airmail, please?
How much is it to send this parcel by airmail?
Can you weigh this for me, please?
How much will it cost to send this by surface mail?
How long will it take?

Speak up!

2 Imagine you are in a post office. Use the ideas below to ask questions.

Example: a
You say: I'd like to send a letter to Oman, please.

a send  → Oman

b buy 7 × 72p

c 3 × → Italy / cost?

d  → South Africa / surface mail / cost?

e  → Portugal / air mail / how long?

f  weigh? / → Canada / cost?

3 🔊32 Now listen to a post office clerk. Use the ideas below to have a conversation.

Example:
You hear: How can I help you?
       a
You say: I'd like to send this parcel to Japan, please.

a send / parcel / Japan
b No, not urgent
c How long / take / surface mail?
d OK / how much / airmail?
e How long / take / airmail?
f OK / send / airmail

F Speaking – Changing money

Speaking strategy: Accepting or declining a service

1 🎧 **33** Listen to conversations a–d and notice the expressions in **bold**.

a The commission is 2%.
   That's fine. Can I change some dollars, please?
b We charge £3.50 commission.
   Hmm. **I'll think about it, thanks**.
c One euro will get you 67 pence.
   Yes, that's OK. Here's my passport.
d One US dollar is 109 Japanese yen.
   I think I'll leave it, thank you.

2 **Which two expressions do you use**

a to accept a service _That's fine,_ ....
b to decline a service ....

Speak up!

3 🎧 **34** Now listen to the clerk in e–i and use the ideas below to respond.

Example:
You hear: e
            Today's exchange rate from dollars to euros
            is .75.
You say: That's fine. I'd like to change $100 into euros.

e ✓ $100 → euros
f ✗
g ✓ £200 → dollars
h ✗
i ✓ €100 → pounds

Class bonus

Work with a partner.
Student A: You are a customer in a bank. Decide what
            services you want, then ask the clerk.
Student B: You are a bank clerk. Answer the customer's
            questions.
Then swap roles and role play a different conversation in
a post office.

E✗tra practice

Go to a bureau de change. The person working there
should be able to speak English. Ask to speak to them
in English, and explain that you want to practise. If they
agree, ask about the commission, the exchange rate for
various currencies, and perhaps change a small amount
of money!

Can-do checklist

Tick what you can do.

	Can do	Need more practice
I can ask about and understand services in a bank.		
I can send different types of mail in a post office.		
I can ask about services and accept or decline them.		
I can change money, ask about exchange rates and commission.		

Unit 6
I don't feel very well

Get ready to listen and speak

- Tick ✓ the things you do to keep healthy.

  take regular exercise ☐   eat fresh fruit and vegetables ☐   drink a lot of water ☐

- When was the last time you were ill?

  a week ago ☐   a month ago ☐   six months ago ☐   a year ago ☐

- Match each health problem (a–h) with a picture (1–8).

  a a cough _4_   b a cold _____   c a sore throat _____   d a temperature _____
  e a headache _____   f backache _____   g a toothache _____   h sunburn _____

go to Useful language p. 80

A Listening – Health problems

1 🔊35 **Listen and complete these three conversations.**

a
What's the _____matter_____ ?
I don't _____ very well. I've got a bad _____ .
Oh, dear. I'm _____ to hear that.

b
_____ wrong?
My back _____ .
_____ you!

c
Are you _____ OK?
Not really. I think I've got a _____ .
I hope you feel _____ soon.

2 🔊35 **Listen and check. Then look at the conversations. Find three expressions to write in each column below.**

asking about someone's health	explaining a health problem	showing sympathy
What's the matter?		

B Speaking – Talking about health problems

Speaking strategy: Showing sympathy

1 You can use these expressions to show sympathy when someone is ill.

Oh, dear. I'm sorry to hear that.
Poor you! How awful.
I hope you feel better soon.

Speak up!

2 🔊 **36** Listen to these six people tell you about a health problem. Reply to each person, showing sympathy.

Example:
You hear: a
              I walked home last night in the rain and now
              I have a really bad cold.
You say: Oh dear. I'm sorry to hear that.

Focus on ... 🔍
giving advice

Complete each sentence using *should* or *shouldn't.*

When you feel very ill you …
.... see a doctor.
.... take some medicine.
.... continue to work.
.... go home and rest.

To keep healthy you …
.... drink lots of water.
.... smoke.
.... eat fresh fruit and vegetables.
.... exercise regularly.
.... eat a lot of fried food.

C Speaking – At the chemist's

Speaking strategy: Asking about medication

1 You can use the expressions in **bold** to ask about medication at the chemist's.

Have you got something for sunburn?
How many tablets should I take?
What have you got for a headache?
How much cream should I use?
How often should I use the cream?

Speak up!

2 Look at the pictures. Imagine you are at the chemist's and you have these health problems. Ask for medication.

Example: a
You say: Excuse me. Have you got something for
             toothache?

3 🔊 **37** Imagine you are at the chemist's. Listen to the chemist and use the ideas below to have conversations.

Example:
You hear: a
              Hello. Can I help you?
You say: Yes. Have you got something for backache?
You hear: Yes, you can try this cream. It's very good.
You say: OK, great. How much should I use?
You hear: Just a small amount, twice a day.

a backache / how much?
b a sore throat / how many?
c a temperature / how often?
d a cough / how much?
e sunburn / how much?

Did you know …?

In Australia and South Africa, people go to the *pharmacy*. In British English many people say *chemist's* and in American English people say *drugstore.*

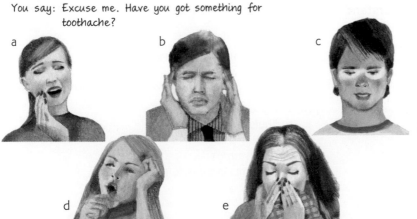

a   b   c

d   e

D Listening – Making an appointment

1 🔊 38 **Adli, from Saudi Arabia, and Fernando, from Brazil, are phoning to make a doctor's appointment. Listen to each conversation and complete the information.**

	Day	Time	Doctor
Adli	Thursday	....	....
Fernando	....	....	Williams

2 **Can you remember how Fernando asks for an appointment? Complete the expression below.**

.... an appointment, please.

Learning tip

Focus your listening. Listen only for the information you need. For example, listen for days, times, and names.

Sound smart
the schwa /ə/

The schwa is a weak sound. It is pronounced /ə/. It is very common in spoken English.

1 🔊 39 Notice the schwas in these words. Listen and repeat.
doct**o**r wat**er** pharm**a**cy tabl**e**t symp**a**thy

2 🔊 39 Underline the schwas in these words. Listen and repeat.
problem important conversation patient temperature

3 🔊 39 Notice the schwas in these sentences. Listen and repeat.
H**a**ve **you** got something **for a** headache?
Wh**a**t h**a**ve **you** got **for a** sore throat?

4 🔊 39 Underline the schwas in these sentences. Listen and repeat.
Take regular exercise.   I was ill a week ago.
Can I make an appointment, please?

E Speaking – Confirming an appointment

Speaking strategy: Checking important details

1 <u>Underline</u> **the expression that Adli and Fernando both use to check they understand important details.**

Adli: So that's Doctor Brown on Thursday at 10.30.
Receptionist: That's right.

Fernando: So that's Wednesday at 3pm, with Doctor Williams.
Receptionist: Yes, that's fine.

Speak up!

2 🔊 40 **Listen to the doctor's receptionist and use the ideas below to make an appointment. Use your own name, and check the details using So that's ... .**

Example:
You hear: Hello. Doctor Park's surgery.
                                    a
You say: Hello. I'd like to make an appointment, please.

a make / appointment
b Thursday afternoon
c ✓
d (*your name*)
e confirm: Doctor Park, Thursday, 4:30

Focus on ...
imperatives

ab **c** def

1 Look at these sentences that doctors often use to give advice to a patient. Notice the imperatives in **bold.** How do you make the imperative?
   + **Drink** a lot of water.
   – **Don't eat** unhealthy food.

2 Use these verbs in the imperative to complete each sentence.
   use   work   try   take   stay   go   drink

   a .... one tablet twice a day.
   b .... to work this week.
   c .... in bed for a few days.
   d .... too much coffee.
   e .... this cream every night.
   f .... to relax and rest.
   g .... too hard.

F Listening – At the doctor's

(41) **Imagine you are at the doctor's, and the doctor is giving you advice. Listen to three doctors and tick ✓ True or False.**

		True	False
a			
1	You've got a bad cold.	☐	✓
2	You should take two tablets twice a day.	☐	☐
3	You should drink lots of water.	☐	☐
b			
1	The doctor is not sure why you have backache.	☐	☐
2	You should put some cream on every morning.	☐	☐
3	You should go back to the doctor's in two weeks.	☐	☐
c			
1	You've got the flu.	☐	☐
2	You should stay in bed and rest.	☐	☐
3	You shouldn't work for three days.	☐	☐

Did you know ...?
The real name for *the flu* is in**flu**enza.

Class bonus
Half the class are doctors, the other half are patients.
Patients: Decide what's wrong with you (*a bad cold, backache*, etc.). Go to see different doctors and explain your problem. Which doctor gives the best advice?
Doctors: Speak to various patients. Find out what's the matter with them, show sympathy and give some advice.

E X tra practice
Imagine you are ill. Make a list of your symptoms and then imagine you are at the doctor's. Tell the doctor what is wrong. If possible, record what you say and listen to yourself afterwards. Can you identify any areas you could improve (for example, your grammar, pronunciation, etc.)?

Can-do checklist

Tick what you can do.

	Can do	Need more practice
I can explain common health problems.		
I can make an appointment and confirm important details.		
I can ask for medication and understand basic instructions.		
I can express sympathy and give advice on health problems.		

Unit 7
Your passport, please

go to Useful language p. 80

Get ready to listen and speak

● Write the number of each item (a–f) next to the correct picture (1–6).
- a a passport
- b a boarding card
- c a visa
- d a flight number
- e hand luggage
- f a suitcase/bag

● Match each verb (a–e) with an expression (1–5).
- a pack
- b queue
- c go to
- d show
- e board

- 1 your boarding card
- 2 the plane
- 3 at the check-in desk
- 4 the gate
- 5 your bags

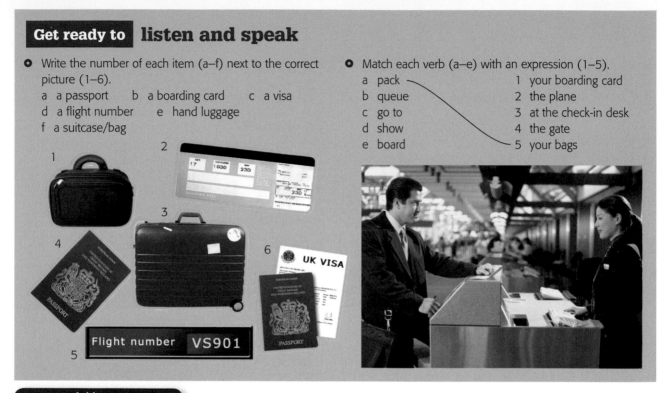

A Listening – At the check-in desk

1 Da-Ho is at London Heathrow airport. Before you listen to his conversation at the check-in desk, look at the questions and guess which words are missing.

- a Can I have your ____ticket____ and _____ , please?
- b Did you _____ your _____ yourself?
- c How many bags are you _____ in?
- d Are there any sharp items in your _____ ?
- e Would you like an aisle seat or a _____ seat?

2 🔊42 Now listen to the conversation and complete the questions in Exercise 1.

3 🔊42 Listen again and answer these questions.
- a When does the flight leave?   ____at 1:20____
- b What Gate does Da-Ho need to go to?   _____
- c What time should he go to the gate?   _____

Learning tip

It is sometimes possible to guess what someone is going to say *before* they say it – especially in situations where people use the same language every time (e.g. checking in at an airport or hotel).

Did you know ...?

The largest airport in the world is King Khalid International Airport in Riyadh, Saudi Arabia. It covers 81 square miles. London Heathrow, the busiest international airport in the world, covers less than 5 square miles.

B Speaking – Providing information

Speaking strategy: Responding to requests

1 (42) **You can use these expressions when you give something to someone. Listen again to Da-Ho's conversation and tick ✓ the expressions you hear.**

a Here it is.
b Here they are.
c Here you are.
d Here you go. *(informal)*

Speak up!

2 (43) **Imagine you are checking in at London Heathrow airport. Listen to the check-in clerk and use the ideas below to answer each question. Use the expressions in Exercise 1 where possible.**

Example:
You hear: a
          Hello. Can I have your passport, please?
You say: Yes, here it is.

a ✓
b ✓
c ✓
d 2
e ✓ 1 bag
f ✗
g Window

C Listening – Going through immigration

1 (44) **Da-Ho is arriving at Los Angeles International airport. He is speaking to an immigration officer. Listen and number the questions in the order you hear them (1–5).**

...... Where are you going to stay?
...... What's the purpose of your visit?
..1.. Where are you travelling from today?
...... How long are you going to stay in the country?
...... Do you have anything to declare?

2 (44) **Tick ✓ True or False for each statement. Then listen again and check.**

		True	False
a	Da-Ho is in Los Angeles on holiday.	☐	✓
b	He's got a meeting tomorrow.	☐	☐
c	He has nothing to declare.	☐	☐
d	He's going to stay with some friends.	☐	☐
e	He's going to stay for a week.	☐	☐

D Speaking – Answering questions

Speaking strategy: Giving clear answers

1 Look at some of Da-Ho's answers to the immigration officer.

Where are you travelling from today?
From London.
Where are you going to stay?
At the Orlando Hotel.

a Does Da-Ho use full sentences? YES / NO
b Are his answers short? YES / NO
c Are his answers clear? YES / NO

When you are giving information to an official, give short, clear answers.

Speak up!

2 🔊 **445** Imagine you are talking to an immigration officer. Use the ideas below to answer the immigration officer's questions.

Example:
You hear: a
       Where are you travelling from today?
You say: From Cairo.

a from Cairo   b business   c nothing
d Hilton Hotel   e 2 weeks

E Speaking – At the Information desk

Speaking strategy: Asking for information

1 <u>Underline</u> the expressions you can use to ask for information.

Excuse me. <u>Where can I get</u> a taxi, please?
Where can I hire a car?
Where can I find a bureau de change?
Where's the bus station, please?
How can I get to the city centre?
Can you recommend a good hotel?

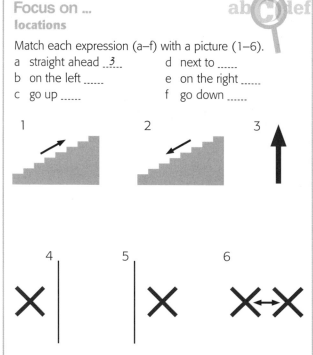

Focus on ...
locations

Match each expression (a–f) with a picture (1–6).
a straight ahead __3__   d next to ......
b on the left ......   e on the right ......
c go up ......   f go down ......

1   2   3

4   5   6

Speak up!

2 Imagine you are at an information desk at an airport. Use the ideas below and ask for information.

Example: a
You say: Where can I get a bus to the city centre?

a  → city centre?

b change money?
c bus station?

d  ?

e recommend / city centre?

f 🚕 ?

Learning tip

When you want to get someone's attention, it is important to be polite. Do not immediately ask your question, but begin by saying *Excuse me.* To be very polite, you can say *Excuse me. I wonder if you can help me.*

F Listening – At the meeting point

1 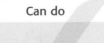 Listen to two conversations at an airport Arrivals hall. Match each conversation (a or b) to the correct picture (1 or 2).

MEETING POINT

1 ☐

Mrs. Hatano

2 ☐

2 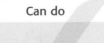 Listen again to the language the people use. Make notes.

	to greet each other	to make an offer	to say thank you
Conversation a	*Pleased to meet you.*	....	....
Conversation b	....	....	....

3 Which conversation is:

informal ......   formal ......

Class bonus

With your partner, role play different conversations at an airport.

Student A: You are a clerk at an airport check-in desk. Ask the passenger questions and check their passport.

Student B: You are an airline passenger. Answer the questions and show your passport.

Then swap roles and role play a different conversation at the information desk and immigration.

E X tra practice

Listen again to recording 45 from section D. Imagine you are going through immigration and a customs officer stops you to ask some questions. This time, answer each question using your own ideas.

Can-do checklist

Tick what you can do.

	Can do	Need more practice
I can check in at an airport and go through immigration.		
I can provide information and give clear answers.		
I can ask for information about transport, facilities, etc.		
I can greet friends and people I don't know.		

Unit 8
A single room, please

go to Useful language p. 81

Get ready to listen and speak

- Do you travel often? ☺ Yes, often. ☺ Sometimes. ☹ No, hardly ever.

- When you are away from home, where do you think is the best place to stay?
  at large hotels ☐   at small friendly hotels ☐   at a bed & breakfast ☐   with friends ☐

A Listening – Making a reservation

1 🔊47 **Listen to these sentences. Who do you think is speaking? Tick ✓ Receptionist or Guest.**

	Receptionist	Guest
a	☐	✓
b	☐	☐
c	☐	☐
d	☐	☐
e	☐	☐
f	☐	☐
g	☐	☐
h	☐	☐

2 🔊48 **Juan Carlos is travelling in Germany. He goes into a hotel in Berlin to book a room. Listen to the conversation and complete each question he asks.**

a How much is a ___single room___ , please?
b Do you have any _____ ?
c Are the rooms _____ ?
d Is _____ included?
e How far is it to the _____ from here?

3 🔊48 **Now listen again and write the answer to each question (a–e).**

a __€60__   b _____   c _____   d _____   e _____

B Speaking – At the check-in desk

Speaking strategy: Confirming details

1 Look at the conversations. Notice how the guest turns a statement into a question to check details.

Guest: The room's got a view, hasn't it?
Receptionist: Yes, that's right.

Guest: Breakfast is included, isn't it?
Receptionist: Yes, that's correct.

Speak up!

2 Number each line of this conversation in order (1–5).

..... Thank you. It's a non-smoking room, isn't it?
..... Good. And breakfast starts at 6.30, doesn't it?
..... Yes, 6.30, that's right. Enjoy your stay.
..... Yes, that's correct. All our rooms are non-smoking.
..1.. Here's your room key. Your room is 254.

3 (149) Listen and check. Then listen again. Pause the recording and repeat the guest's words.

4 Imagine you are going to stay in a hotel. Use the ideas below to check details about your booking.

Example: a
You say: It's a non-smoking room, isn't it?

a non-smoking room?
b breakfast included?
c on the first floor?
d dinner starts at eight?
e a single room?
f got a shower?

Learning tip

When you speak in English, don't worry about making mistakes. Keep talking! Don't stop to think or try to translate what to say in your head.

Focus on ...
making statements into questions

Make each statement a question by adding *hasn't it?* or *isn't it?*

a It's a double room, ____isn't it?____
b It's got a bath, _____
c My booking is for three nights, _____
d My room's on the ground floor, _____
e The room's got a mini bar, _____
f The check-out time is eleven o'clock, _____
g The room's got a TV, _____

Did you know ...?

People describe which floor of a building you're on in different ways in different countries.

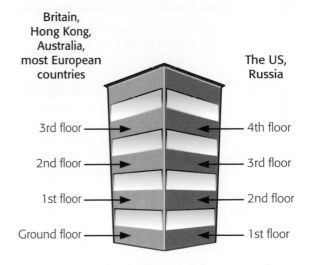

Britain, Hong Kong, Australia, most European countries

The US, Russia

3rd floor — 4th floor
2nd floor — 3rd floor
1st floor — 2nd floor
Ground floor — 1st floor

C Listening – Describing your room

1 🔊 **50 Listen to four people each describe their hotel room. Match each person (a–d) with a room (1–4).**

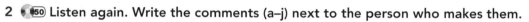

a Z
b ☐

Aiko

Ulrike

c ☐
d ☐

Rashid

Marc

2 🔊 **50 Listen again. Write the comments (a–j) next to the person who makes them.**

a It has a bath and a shower.
b It's a bit small.
c There's also a hair dryer, and an iron and ironing board.
d There's a nice view over the park.
e The TV has lots of movie channels.
f It's pretty big and there's a nice balcony.
g The bed's huge.
h I can make tea and coffee, too.
i There's a mini-bar.
j The air-conditioning is really good.

Aiko ....

Ulrike ....

Rashid ....

Marc ....

D Listening – Hotel facilities and services

1 🔊 **51 John from London is checking into a hotel in Brazil. He asks about facilities in the hotel. Listen to the receptionist and tick ✓ the facilities that she mentions.**

café ✓   restaurant ☐   swimming pool ☐   fitness centre ☐
bar ☐   gift shop ☐   business centre ☐   car parking ☐

2 🔊 **51 Listen again and tick ✓ True or False for each statement.**

	True	False
a Breakfast is from 7.30 to ten every morning.	☐	✓
b The café is next to the gift shop.	☐	☐
c There is an Italian restaurant on the fourth floor.	☐	☐
d The bar closes at 2am.	☐	☐
e The fitness centre is on the ground floor.	☐	☐

3 🔊 **52 Read the questions that John asks. Then listen again to the replies the receptionist gives. Write the number of each question (a–f) next to the correct reply (1–6).**

a Do you have internet access here?
b Can I have a wake-up call?
c Is room service available?
d When's the check-out time?
e Do you have a laundry service?
f Can I have a newspaper in the morning, please?

1 _d_   2 ......   3 ......
4 ......   5 ......   6 ......

E Speaking – Dealing with problems

Speaking strategy: Making a complaint

1 You can use the expressions in **bold** to complain about your room.

Sorry to bother you, but there's no towel in my room.
I'm afraid that the light in my room doesn't work.
Sorry, but my room is too cold.

Speak up!

2 Imagine you are a guest in a hotel. Look at these problems and think of what you can say. Then complain to the hotel manager. Speak your answers.

Example: a
You say: Sorry, but my room is very noisy. I think someone is playing
music next door.

3 Now look at these problems and complain to the hotel manager. Speak your answers.

a There's no hot water in your bathroom.
b You asked for a room with a bath, but there is only a shower.
c The television doesn't work.
d The bathroom is dirty and the toilet won't flush.
e You ordered a meal from room service an hour ago, but you are still waiting.

Sound smart
/djə/

1 ●53 Listen and notice the way *do* and *you* are linked.

Do you /djə/ have internet access?
What time do you /djə/ serve breakfast?
Do you /djə/ have any non-smoking rooms?
What restaurants do you /djə/ have?
Do you /djə/ have a room with a view?

2 ●53 Listen again and repeat each sentence. Practise the pronunciation of /djə/.

Class bonus

Make a group of three. Each choose one of the characters below. Decide why the guest is unhappy, and plan a conversation. Practise first, then role play your conversation to the class.
an unhappy hotel guest
a manager   a receptionist

E**X**tra practice

Phone a large international hotel in your area. Ask about the facilities and services they have. Speak in English and use the language in this unit to help you.

Can-do checklist

Tick what you can do.

	Can do	Need more practice
I can ask about services and facilities in a hotel.		
I can make a reservation in a hotel.		
I can check into a hotel and talk about my room.		
I can make a complaint about common problems in a hotel.		

Unit 9
When is the next train?

Get ready to listen and speak

- How often do you use public transport?
  every day ☐   quite often ☐   not very often ☐

- Match each type of transport (a–h) with a picture (1–8).
  Which do you like to use?
  a train   b coach   c bus   d metro
  e car   f bicycle   g taxi   h tram

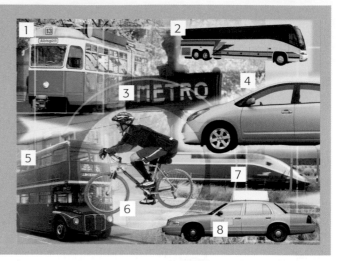

go to Useful language p. 81

A Speaking – At the train station

Speaking strategy: Buying a ticket

1 Stephen is buying a ticket at Singapore airport.
Complete the conversation using these questions.

Can I have a single to the city centre, please?
How long does it take?
What time's the next train?
Which platform does it leave from?

Clerk: Next, please.
Stephen: a *Can I have a single to the city centre, please?*
Clerk: A single? Of course, here you are.
Stephen: b _____
Clerk: Usually about thirty minutes.
Stephen: c _____
Clerk: The next train's at 3.15.
Stephen: d _____
Clerk: Platform 3. Over there.
Stephen: Thank you.
Clerk: You're welcome.

Speak up!

2 🔘 54 Listen and check. Then listen again. Pause
the recording after Stephen speaks, and
repeat his words.

3 🔘 55 Imagine you are at London King's Cross
station. Listen to the ticket clerk and use the
ideas below to have a conversation.

Example:
You hear: Next, please.
                    a
You say: I'd like a return ticket to Cambridge, please.

a return ticket / Cambridge
b how much?
c how long / take?
d next train?
e which platform?

42   💻 Social and Travel

B Listening – Times

1 🔊 **156 Listen to announcements a–d and complete the information.**

King's Cross station		
Train to	**Time**	**Platform**
a Edinburgh	7.45	
b York		
c Cambridge		
d Liverpool		

Did you know …?

In the UK, the metro is called the *underground* or the *tube*. In the USA it is called the *subway*.

2 🔊 **156 Listen to announcements e–j. Match each announcement (e–j) to the correct time (1–6).**

1   2   3

4   5   6

e _2_   f _____   g _____   h _____   i _____   j _____

3 🔊 **157 Stacey works in South Africa. Look at her diary and listen to her talk about her day. Write the times in the diary.**

a breakfast with Mrs Jenson (ALC) _____8:30_____

b meeting with Bob/Sean
_____

c see Helen re sales report
_____

d lunch with Dan Chester
_____

e GEO International
_____

f collect Janet from school
_____

Focus on …
understanding the time

1   Look at three different ways you can say the time in English.

12:10

a *ten past twelve*
b *ten minutes past twelve*
c *twelve ten*

In American English people also say *ten after twelve*.

2   Match the times (1–8) to the clocks (a–h).
1   a quarter past ten   ____h____
2   twenty-five to nine   _____
3   seven twenty   _____
4   a quarter to two   _____
5   ten past four   _____
6   twelve thirty   _____
7   nine fifty-five   _____
8   twelve twenty-five   _____

3   Now look at the times below. Say each one.

a   b   c   d

e   f   g   h

C Listening – Following directions

1 🔊**58** **Listen to conversations a and b and complete these directions.**

a You go _____*along*_____ Nether Street and
   _____ .

b You turn _____ and go _____ the bank. The subway's _____ .

2 🔊**58** **Look at the map and listen to conversations c–f. Follow the directions and write the name of each place you arrive at. Begin at *You are here*.**

c ___*post office*_____

d _____

e _____

f _____

Focus on ...
giving directions

Use the words below to complete the expressions for giving directions.

miss   along   on   far   turn   past

a Go _____*along*_____ this road.

b _____ right/left by the traffic lights.

c Go _____ the bank.

d It's _____ your right/left.

e It's not _____ .

f You can't _____ it.

Sound smart
Intonation

You can repeat important information back to someone to check that it is correct. Make your voice go up at the end to make a question.

1 🔊**59** Listen to these two short conversations. Notice how B's voice goes up at the end to check.

A: Go along here and turn left. The bus station is on the corner.
B: On the corner?
A: Yes.

A: The post office is past the bank on the left.
B: OK, so past the bank on the left?
A: Yes.

2 Say each expression below as a question, making your voice go up at the end.
   a At 10 o'clock?   b On the left?
   c It leaves in three minutes?   d At 4.15?
   e On Park Road?

3 🔊**60** Listen to these statements and reply. Check the important information by repeating it as a question.

Example:
You hear: a
             Go along here and turn left. The train station's on the right.
You say: On the right?

D Speaking – Finding your way

Speaking strategy: Asking for and giving directions

1 <u>Underline</u> the expressions you can use to ask for directions.

Excuse me. <u>Where's the</u> bus station, please?
Excuse me. I'm lost. How do I get to the Art Museum?
Can you tell me where the Beach Hotel is, please?

Speak up!

2 **Rearrange the words to make questions asking for directions.**

a you / me / tell / where / library / Can / the / is / please
   .Can you tell me where the library is, please.. ?

b get / to / city / How / I / centre / do /the
   .... ?

c Tourist / Where's / please / Office / the / Information
   .... ?

d the / hospital / me / tell / where / Can / please / you / is
   .... ?

3 **Imagine you are lost. Ask for directions to these places.**

Example: a
You say: Can you tell me where the cinema is, please?

a the cinema
b the train station
c the internet café
d the nearest supermarket
e the Tourist Information Office

4 ⊙ **61 Look at the map on page 44. Imagine you are at *You are here*. Listen to five people ask for directions. Pause the recording after each one and give directions to the place.**

Example:
You hear: a
        Can you tell me where the subway is, please?
You say: You turn right into Broadway, then turn left into Willow Way.
        It's on the left.

Learning tip

Try to *think* in English as much as possible. Whenever you have some free time, think of what you can say in different situations. For example, imagine a tourist stops you in the street and asks you a question. What could they ask? How could you answer?

E✗tra practice

Go to the BBC *Learning English* website and type 'train listen' in the search box. Press enter, then click on a link that interests you. Find something to watch or listen to, and complete any exercises. http://www.bbc.co.uk/worldservice/learningenglish

Class bonus

Work with a partner. Look at the map on page 44. Choose a place to start, then take turns asking for and giving directions to other places on the map.

Can-do checklist

Tick what you can do.

	Can do	Need more practice
I can ask about travel details.		
I can understand the time.		
I can ask for and give directions.		
I can check information to make sure I understand.		

Unit 10
There's so much to see!

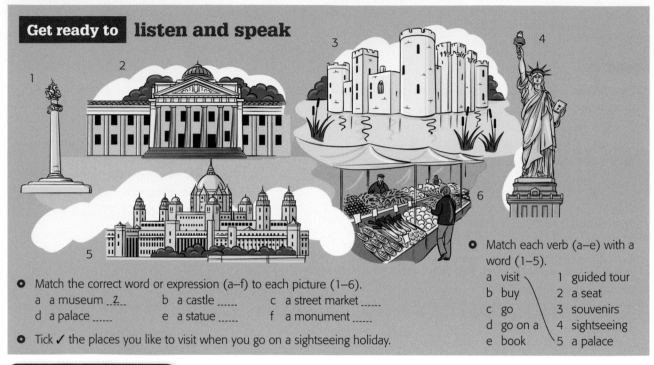

Get ready to listen and speak

○ Match the correct word or expression (a–f) to each picture (1–6).
   a a museum _2_   b a castle _____   c a street market _____
   d a palace _____   e a statue _____   f a monument _____

○ Match each verb (a–e) with a word (1–5).
   a visit   1 guided tour
   b buy   2 a seat
   c go   3 souvenirs
   d go on a   4 sightseeing
   e book   5 a palace

○ Tick ✓ the places you like to visit when you go on a sightseeing holiday.

go to Useful language p. 80

A Listening – At a Tourist Information Office

1 🔊 62 James is visiting Hong Kong. He is at a Tourist Information Office. Listen and complete the questions he asks. Then listen and repeat.

   a Are there any good ____markets____ here?
   b What _____ do you recommend?
   c Where's the best place to _____ ?
   d Are there any _____ I can visit near here?
   e Is there a _____ I can go on?

2 🔊 63 Now listen to the assistant in the Tourist Information Office and match each answer (1–5) with a question (a–e).

   1 _d_   2 _____   3 _____   4 _____   5 _____

Focus on ...
there is/there are

Complete each sentence with *There's a, There are, Is there a...* or *Are there any...*
   a _Is there a_____ market near here?
   b _____ large castle in the town.
   c _____ good shops?
   d _____ some large parks.
   e _____ theatre?
   f _____ two art galleries.
   g _____ monuments worth seeing?
   h _____ 12th Century bridge.

Class bonus

1 Make a list of interesting things to see in your home town.
2 Work with a partner.
   Student A: Imagine you work in a Tourist Information Office. Answer your partner's questions.
   Student B: You are a tourist in your partner's home town. Find out what there is to do.
   When you have finished, swap roles.

B Listening – Planning your visit

1 🔊 **64 Listen to Jim and Denise talk about what to do in New York. Tick ✓ the places that they mention.**

the Statue of Liberty ☐   the Metropolitan Museum of Art ✓   Central Park ☐
the Guggenheim Museum ☐   the Empire State Building ☐   Times Square ☐

2 🔊 **64 Listen again. Which three places do they decide to go to?**

Did you know …?

People from New York are called *New Yorkers*. American jazz players in the 1930s called a city an *apple*. Of course, New York was *The Big Apple*. Many people still use this name today.

C Speaking – Deciding what to do

Speaking strategy: Making and responding to suggestions

1 **Look at these extracts from Jim and Denise's conversation. Underline the expressions they use to make suggestions.**

Why don't we go to the Statue of Liberty?
How about going to the Metropolitan Museum of Art?
What about going to Central Park?
Let's go there first.

2 **You can use these expressions to respond to a suggestion. Match each group of expressions a–c to a meaning 1–3.**

a That's a good idea.   That sounds great.   That's fine with me.
b It's up to you.   I don't mind.
c I'd rather not do that today.   I don't really want to do that.
   I'd rather do something else.

1 I don't agree. _c_
2 You can choose. _____
3 I agree. _____

3 🔊 **64 Listen again to Jim and Denise's conversation. Tick ✓ the expressions from Exercise 2 that you hear.**

Speak up!

4 **Imagine you are visiting New York with a friend. Suggest visiting these places. Speak your answers.**

Example: a
You say: *How about going to the Statue of Liberty?*

a the Statue of Liberty
b the Guggenheim Museum
c the Empire State Building
d the Metropolitan Museum of Art
e Central Park
f Times Square

D Listening – Looking around

1 🔊 65 Bill and Giulia are sightseeing around Sydney, Australia. Listen and number the attractions (1–5) in the order Bill and Giulia mention them.

2 🔊 65 Listen again and write the number of the correct attraction next to each fact.

a This is where the first white people arrived in Australia in 1788. __1__

b You can get a great view from here. ......

c It opened in 1973. ......

d You can go on a guided walking tour. ......

e It's one of the biggest in the world. ......

3 🔊 65 Look at these expressions you can use to react to something you see. Listen again and tick ✓ the expressions you hear.

It's great!   It's wonderful!   How amazing!
It's huge!   How beautiful!   It's fantastic!

Sound smart
Using stress to respond to suggestions

1 🔊 66 Listen to these sentences and notice the stress on the underlined words.

That's a <u>good</u> idea.   I <u>don't mind</u>.
That sounds <u>great</u>.   It's <u>up</u> to <u>you</u>.
I <u>don't really</u> want to <u>do</u> that.   That's <u>fine</u> with <u>me</u>.
I'd <u>rather</u> do something <u>else</u>.   That sounds <u>fun</u>.

2 🔊 66 Listen again and repeat. Try to copy the same stress.

Focus on ...
adjectives

1 Match the opposites.

beautiful   crowded
cheap   dangerous
quiet   boring
relaxing   ugly
clean   stressful
safe   expensive
lively   dirty

2 Write the adjectives in the correct column, Positive or Negative.

wonderful terrible awful fantastic marvellous disappointing dreadful great amazing disgusting

Positive	Negative
wonderful	terrible
....	....
....	....
....	....
....	....

E Listening – A guided tour

1 🔊 **67** Look at the map and listen to this tour guide on a tour bus in Barcelona. Which route does the bus take? _____

2 🔊 **67** Listen again and tick ✓ True or False for each statement.

	True	False
a Las Ramblas is two kilometres long.	✓	☐
b Gaudí only designed the furniture in Casa Battlo.	☐	☐
c Casa Milà was originally a police station.	☐	☐
d Casa Milà was built in 1910.	☐	☐
e Work on the Sagrada Familia began in 1882.	☐	☐
f Gaudí died before the cathedral was finished.	☐	☐

F Speaking – Talking about your experiences

Speaking strategy: Describing places you know

1 You can use these expressions to describe a place you are visiting.

The people are very friendly.	It's very quiet.
The food is great.	It's quite expensive.
The hotel is a bit disappointing.	There's a lot to see.

E X tra practice

Think of an English-speaking country you would like to visit, and find out what you can see and do on holiday there. Watch a travel programme about it in English on satellite or cable TV. Listen to a radio programme in English about going on holiday there. Contact the nearest official Tourist Informatin Office and ask if they have any video material to watch in English. There may also be lectures you can go to for more information.

Speak up!

2 Imagine you are visiting Barcelona. Use the ideas below to talk about the city. Use the adjectives in Focus on ... to help you.

Example: a
You say: The food is OK. It's quite nice.

a food ☺ b people ☺ c night life ☺
d prices ☹ e hotel ☹ f things to see ☺
g beach ☺

3 Think of a place you know well. Describe it, using the words and expressions above to help you.

Learning tip

If possible, record yourself speaking. Then listen and think about things you can improve. Is your pronunciation clear? Can you hear any errors?

Can-do checklist

Tick what you can do.

	Can do	Need more practice
I can ask for basic information at a Tourist Information Office.		
I can make and respond to suggestions.		
I can ask follow a guided tour.		
I can talk about places I visit on holiday.		

Review 1
Units 1–10

Section 1

🎧 **68** **Listen and reply to each statement you hear. Circle your answer.**

1
a Yes, please. How much is this shirt?
b I'm very well, thank you.
c What's the problem?

2
a Yes, you are.
b Yes, I am.
c No, thank you.

3
a I'm fine, thanks.
b Yes, it is, isn't it?
c Pleased to meet you, too.

4
a Sure. Go ahead.
b Oh, not too bad, thanks.
c Yes, I do.

5
a Three, please.
b Yes, please.
c Yes, I would.

6
a No, thank you.
b How about you?
c Yes, here you are.

7
a Nice to meet you.
b I'm here.
c Yes, it is.

8
a I don't mind.
b Me too.
c It's great!

9
a Really?
b Excuse me.
c Yes, of course.

10
a See you later.
b How's it going?
c How are you?

Section 2

🎧 **69** **Read each situation. Then listen and tick ✓ the best answer.**

1 You are in a shop but you don't know where to pay. What do you say?
   a ......   b ......   c ......

2 You want to use your friend's mobile phone. What do you say?
   a ......   b ......   c ......

3 You have a bad cough and decide to go to a chemist. What do you say?
   a ......   b ......   c ......

4 You are at a party but you don't know anyone. Someone is standing next to you. What do you say?
   a ......   b ......   c ......

5 You find some shoes in a shop but decide they are too expensive. What do you say?
   a ......   b ......   c ......

6 You have finished your meal in a restaurant. What do you say?
   a ......   b ......   c ......

7 You go to a bank to deposit a cheque. What do you say?
   a ......   b ......   c ......

8 You want to introduce your colleague Helen to a group of friends. What do you say?
   a ......   b ......   c ......

9 You like a pair of jeans but you think they might be too big. What do you say?
   a ......   b ......   c ......

10 You want to change some money but the commission is too high. What do you say?
   a ......   b ......   c ......

Section 3

Read each situation and circle your answer.

1 What is the best way to introduce yourself at a party?
   a Say hello and give your full name.
   b Say hello and give your first name only.
   c Just say hello.

2 When you want to check important details, should you …
   a wait and then repeat the important information back to the speaker?
   b make notes and check later?
   c interrupt the speaker to ask them to repeat?

3 Which of these expressions can you use to give someone some advice?
   a I think you should …
   b Do you think you could …?
   c Would you mind …?

4 What should you say if someone says a word or expression you don't understand?
   a Sorry, what do you mean?
   b I can't understand what you are saying.
   c Can you speak a bit more slowly, please?

5 Your hotel room is too dark and you call reception. What is the best thing to say?
   a Come and replace the light.
   b Sorry, but the light in my room doesn't work.
   c Please repair the light in here.

6 When an immigration officer asks you for information, should you …
   a reply, then ask a question?
   b answer and give as much detail as possible?
   c give only the information they ask for?

7 You are on a bus. It's hot and you want to open a window. What should you say to the person next to you?
   a Would you mind if I open a window?
   b I want to open a window.
   c I'm going to open this window.

8 A friend suggests going to a museum. Which is the most polite way to say you don't want to go?
   a No, I don't want to do that.
   b I'd rather not do that.
   c That's a terrible idea.

9 Which of these is not a good topic for making small talk?
   a family
   b weather
   c politics

10 Which sentence is most polite?
   a I'll take your bag.
   b Give me your bag.
   c May I take your bag?

Section 4

Read each statement and write a possible reply.

1 Why don't we go to the art gallery?

----

2 I'm afraid we don't accept cheques.

----

3 What would you like for the main course?

----

4 How was your trip?

----

5 I've got a terrible cough.

----

6 You booked a double room for three nights?

----

7 Excuse me. Where's the nearest bank?

----

8 Look. There's the Empire State Building!

----

9 I'm looking forward to the weekend.

----

10 What's the purpose of your visit?

Unit 11
I'll do it straight away

Get ready to listen and speak

○ Look at the pictures. What do you think the people are saying?

1 ☐   2 ☐   3 ☐

go to Useful language p. 82

A Listening – In an electrical shop

1 🔊12 **Rita Avre works in an electrical shop in South Africa. Listen to three conversations and write the number of each conversation (a–c) next to the correct picture above (1–3).**

2 🔊12 **Listen again and tick ✓ the expressions Rita uses to offer help.**

a May I help you? ......   c Would you like some help? ......
b Can I help you? ......   d Do you need any help? ✓

3 🔊12 **Complete these expressions Rita uses to offer help. Then listen again and check.**

a ____Let me____ show you the way.
b .... give you a new catalogue.
c .... show you?

B Speaking – Helping customers

Speaking strategy: Offering help

1 <u>Underline</u> **the expressions you can use to offer help.**

<u>Let me</u> help you.
I'll give you a hand.
Shall I help you?

Speak up!

2 🔊13 **Imagine you work in a shop. Listen to these customers, and use the ideas below to offer them help.**

Example:
You hear: a
         Excuse me. How much are these?
You say: They're $20. Let me give you a new price list.

a $20 / give you a new price list
b don't worry / find another one
c over there / show you the way
d that's OK / get another one
e help you / take it to your car

52 🎧 **Work and Study**

C Listening – Taking short messages

1 (14) **Five colleagues give Rita messages to pass on. Listen and complete her notes.**

a

Charles –
_____call_____

Chris

b

Cynthia – meeting this
pm in _____
(not MRI)

c

Kevin – email this
month's _____
to Chris ASAP.

d

Sue – don't forget
the _____ at
_____ with
Judith.

e

Joseph – give Chris the
_____ for the
store cupboard.

2 (15) **Now listen to Rita pass on each message. Write which message (a–e) she passes on in each conversation (1–5).**

Conversation 1 __d__
Conversation 2 _____
Conversation 3 _____
Conversation 4 _____
Conversation 5 _____

3 (16) **Imagine you are at work. Some colleagues call you and leave messages for these people. Listen and write each message.**

a David __call Mr Brown._____
b Chris _____
c Helen _____
d Lisa _____
e George _____

Learning tip

When you listen and take a message, only note the important information. You don't need to write in complete sentences. Keep it short, and try to use abbreviations.

D Speaking – Helping colleagues

Speaking strategy: Passing on messages

1 **You can use the expressions in bold to pass on messages.**

Chris **wants you to** email the sales report to him.
He **said** it's very important.

Speak up!

2 **Use the notes on the right and the expressions in Exercise 1 to pass on these messages to your boss.**

Example: a
Your note: Steven – call him.
You say: Steven wants you to call him.

Phone messages:

a Steven – call him.

b George – send sales figures to him.

c Mikael (sales department) – phone him.
It's urgent!

d Mr Lee – meet him in conference room
at 2pm. Important!

e production manager – prepare report
for her.

E Listening – Following instructions

1 🔘 Imagine you are at work. Listen to five managers give you some instructions. What does each person want you to do? Complete the missing information.

TO do

a send ___an email___ to Helen. Tell her there's a
_____ next Tuesday ...

b _____ David Green. Ask him to send the
_____

c ask Bob if he can _____

d email _____ at _____ Ask him
to come to next week's _____

e make _____ of the clarkson file by
_____

Class bonus

1 Work with a partner. Give your partner three messages to pass on to other classmates.
2 Listen to the messages your partner wants you to pass on. Take notes.
3 Find the classmates and give each classmate the message.

2 🔘 Listen again. Tick ✓ the expressions you hear.
a Can you ..✓..
b Would you ....
c Could you ....
d Will you ....
e Would you mind ....

F Speaking – Social English

Speaking strategy: Saying goodbye to visitors

1 🔵**1B** **Listen to conversations a and b. Complete these expressions you can use to say goodbye to visitors.**

a A: Well, I'd better go now.
   B: Well, it was ____*great*____ to see you. Thanks very much for _____ .

b A: I have to leave now, I'm afraid.
   B: Well, I _____ to see you again soon. Have a safe _____ .

E✗**tra practice**

Think about a local shop you often go to and make a list of the products and services they supply. Then imagine a friend asks you about the shop. Talk about it, and if possible record what you say. Listen to yourself afterwards. Can you identify any areas you could improve (for example, your grammar, pronunciation, etc.)?

Speak up!

2 🔵**1B** **Now listen to some more visitors (c–f). Use the expressions in Exercise 1 to say goodbye.**

Example:
You hear: c
        I have to go now to catch my train.
You say: OK. Have a safe journey.

Can-do checklist

Tick what you can do.

	Can do	Need more practice
I can offer help to customers.		
I can understand and follow instructions.		
I can take short messages and pass messages on.		
I can politely ask people not to do something.		
I can say goodbye to visitors in a variety of ways.		

Unit 12
When can you deliver?

go to Useful language p. 82

Get ready to listen and speak

- How often do you …

	very often	quite often	not very often
buy something from a mail order catalogue?	☐	☐	☐
go shopping online?	☐	☐	☐
receive a parcel in the post?	☐	☐	☐

A Listening – Asking about products and services

1 🔊 **9** Listen to five people call Hadley Office Supplies. Tick ✓ the things they ask about.

computers ☐	pens ☐	envelopes ☐
desks ✓	notebooks ☐	photocopiers ☐
chairs ☐	printers ☐	files ☐
printer cartridges ☐		

2 🔊 **9** Which things does the company *not* sell?

3 🔊 **10** Now listen to five people ask about services. Complete the questions they ask.

a Do you _____repair_____ computers?
b Can you give me a _____ ?
c Do you _____ for delivery?
d Could you send it by _____ delivery, please?
e When can you _____ ?

4 🔊 **11** Listen to the replies to the questions above. Match each reply (1–5) with a question (a–e).

1 __c__   2 _____   3 _____   4 _____   5 _____

Did you know …?

The largest delivery company in the world is DHL. It employs over 350,000 people.

Focus on …
some/any

Complete the dialogue with *some* or *any*.

a I'm afraid there aren't __any__ envelopes.
b OK. We need to get _____ more.
c I'll order _____ this afternoon.
d Do we have _____ small notebooks?
e No. We need to buy _____ of those, too.

B Speaking – Explaining what you want

Speaking strategy: Making requests

1 <u>Underline</u> the expressions you can use to make a request.

Can you find out the price, please?

Could you call me when the order is ready?

Speak up!

2 Number each line of this conversation in order (1–6).

...... No, that's everything. Can you deliver?

...... Yes, we do. We sell all sizes of paper.

...... Yes, we deliver free of charge.

...... I'd like to order three boxes of A3, please.

..1.. Hello. Do you sell A3 paper?

...... Certainly. Three boxes. Anything else?

3 ⏵**12** **Listen and check. Then listen again. Pause the recording after the customer speaks, and repeat the customer's words.**

Learning tip

When you make a phone call to order something, make sure you have all the information you need. Keep the conversation short and say only what you need to say.

Class bonus

Half the class are shop assistants, the other half are customers.

Shop assistants: You work in an office supplies company. Decide what products you want to sell (e.g. computers, furniture, etc.). What services do you offer (e.g. repair, free delivery)? Prepare to sell your products and services.

Customers: You want to buy some office supplies. Decide what you want to buy, then go to different shop assistants and ask what products and services they have. Try to get a good deal.

4 **Imagine you call an office supplies company. Use the ideas below and make requests.**

Example: a

You say: Do you repair photocopiers? Can you come today?

a  repair? / come today?

b sell? / discount?

c charge? / deliver Tuesday?

d  large? / send special delivery?

e  sell? / price?

5 **Imagine you are in these situations. What will you say? Speak your answers.**

Example: a

You say: Hello. Can you tell me when our delivery will arrive, please?

a You're waiting for an important delivery. Phone the delivery company to ask when it will arrive.

b You go into a car hire company. You want to know their prices.

c The office is very dirty! Call the cleaning company and ask them to come early.

d Mr Matsumoto, an important client, is coming tonight. Ask your colleague to book a hotel room.

e You need some office furniture urgently. Call the supplier to ask when they can deliver.

C Speaking – Discussing services

**Speaking strategy:
Responding to requests**

1 You can use these expressions to respond to requests. Write P (Positive) or N (Negative) next to each expression.

a Sorry, I'm afraid I can't. ..N..
b Sure, no problem. ......
c I'm afraid not. ......
d Yes, that's fine. ......

Speak up!

2 Match the requests (a–e) with the responses (1–5).

a Can you deliver this next Wednesday?
b Could you please reduce the price?
c Could you send this by airmail?
d Can you repair this computer?
e Can you keep this for me until Tuesday?

1 Sorry. We only sell computers. We don't repair them.
2 Yes, that's fine. But only until then.
3 Yes, but it will cost more.
4 Sorry, I'm afraid I can't. The price is fixed.
5 Sure, no problem. Next Wednesday is fine.

3 🔊13 Listen to each request (a–e) and answer with the correct response (1–5).

4 🔊13 Now listen to requests (f–j). Pause after each request and use the ideas below to respond.

Example:
You hear: f
        Could you deliver this next Saturday?
You say: Yes, that's fine. We'll deliver it before midday.

f ✓ / before midday   h ✓ / cost €12 extra   j ✓ / until 5pm
g ✗ / best price   i ✗ / tomorrow

D Listening – Placing an order

🔊14 Nihar is from India. He calls Hadley Office Supplies to place an order. Listen and complete the form.

 **Hadley** Office Supplies

Order Form

Company: ABS Printers

Items	Quantity	Catalogue no.	Price
			each
		Total: (incl. VAT)	

Focus on ...
adjectives

1 Put the letters in the correct order to make opposites of these adjectives.

a reliable   rluenieabl   ....unreliable....
b large   malls   ....
c cheap   pivexesne   ....
d efficient   niffiiceent   ....
e well-made   lydab-dame   ....

2 Complete the chart with the correct comparatives and superlatives.

a large   .....larger.....   .....largest.....
b ....   cheaper   ....
c easy   .... easiest
d reliable   ....
e .... most efficient
f difficult ....

E Listening – Discussing products

1 🔘15 Emily wants to buy a printer. She is discussing which to buy with her friend, Tom. Listen and tick ✓ the printer she decides to buy.

☐ ☐

2 Can you remember what they say about each printer? Try to complete the chart, then listen and check.

	Advantage	Disadvantage
T150:	cheaper	....
X80:	....	....

3 🔘15 Listen and tick ✓ the expression Emily uses to make her choice.

I think I'll get ...... I'd rather have ...... I'd prefer to have ......

F Speaking – Choosing between products

Speaking strategy: Making comparisons

1 You can use these expressions to make comparisons.

I think this one is better.   This one is cheaper.
This one is bigger.   That one is easier to use.
That one is more reliable.   This one is lighter.

Speak up!

2 Compare these computers. What can you say?

Example: The TriStar is more expensive than the Maxi.

TriStar
Screen - 15 inch,
Memory 80GB,
Speed - 1.8Ghz,
Colour – black,
Price $679

Maxi
Screen - 17 inch,
Memory 60GB,
Speed - 2.0Ghz,
Colour – silver,
Price $599

Sound smart
Emphasizing alternatives

1 🔘16 Listen to question a. Notice how the speaker's voice goes up and then down to emphasize the alternatives.

a Do you want the blue one or the black one?

2 🔘16 Listen to questions b–e. Pause the recording and repeat each one. Try to make your voice go up and then down.

b Do you want to pay by cash or credit card?
c Would you like the T150 or the X80?
d Do you want to order one or two?
e Is the delivery date the 5th or the 6th?

E**X**tra practice

Go to the BBC *Learning English* website and type 'office business listen' in the search box. Press enter, then click on a link that interests you. Find something to watch or listen to, and complete any exercises.
http://www.bbc.co.uk/worldservice/learningenglish

Can-do checklist

Tick what you can do.

	Can do	Need more practice
I can ask about products and services.		
I can make and respond to requests.		
I can place an order for a product.		
I can compare products and choose between alternatives.		

Unit 13
I'll put you through

Get ready to listen and speak

- Which of these things do you do most often on the phone?
  make calls ☐   receive calls ☐   take messages ☐

- How do you feel when you leave a voicemail message for someone?

go to Useful language p. 82

A Listening – Making a call

Did you know …?

In many Asian countries people say *hand phone* or *handy phone*. In Australia, India and the UK people say *mobile phone*, or just *mobile*. People say *cell phone* in South Africa and the USA.

1 🔊17 **Jennifer Ratby works in Los Angeles. She is calling Denco Computing and wants to speak to three people. Listen and match the name of each person with the reason for her call (a–c).**

David   a to arrange a meeting
Kevin   b to discuss next year's prices
Charles   c to ask about the contract

2 🔊17 **Try to answer to these questions from memory. Then listen and check.**

a Who do you think Paul is? _____
b When does David say he'll send the contract? _____
c Why can't Jennifer speak to Charles? _____
d Why can't she speak to Kevin? _____
e What message does she leave for Kevin? _____

Focus on …
telephoning

Choose one word to complete each sentence.

leave   calling   busy   hold
put   call   have   speak

a Can I _____ have _____ extension 726, please?
b Who's _____ , please?
c Would you like to _____ a message?
d Can you _____ the line, please?
e Can I _____ to George Martin, please?
f I'll _____ you through.
g Sorry, the line's _____ at the moment.
h Could you _____ back later?

B Speaking – Problems understanding

Speaking strategy: Making sure you understand

1 Write the words in the correct order to complete these expressions.

a please? / Can / you / Sorry. / repeat / that
   Sorry. Can you repeat that, please?

b I'm / didn't / afraid / quite / I / catch / that.
   ----

c How / Sorry. / spell / that? / do / you
   ----

d please? / slowly, / Can / speak / a bit / you / more
   ----

2 Now match each expression a–d with a situation in which you might use it.

1 When someone says a name or address you don't know. ___c___
2 When someone speaks very quickly. -----------
3 When you don't hear something very well. -----------
4 When you want someone to repeat something. -----------

Sound smart
Spelling names

1 🔊 **19** Listen and repeat these sounds.
   /ei/   /iː/   /e/   /ai/   /əu/   /uː/   /aː/

2 🔊 **19** Now listen to all the letters of the alphabet in order and complete the table below. Then listen and check.

/ei/	/iː/	/e/	/ai/	/əu/	/uː/	/aː/
_a_	------	------	------	------	------	------
------	------	------	------		------	
------	------	------			------	
------	------	------				
	------	------				
	------	------				
	------	------				
	------					

3 🔊 **20** Listen to five people spell their names. Write their names.
   a _____Henman_____
   b --------------------------------
   c --------------------------------
   d --------------------------------
   e --------------------------------

4 🔊 **20** Now look at the names below. Spell each one aloud. Then listen and check.
   f Bradshaw   g Navykarn   h Sukrishna   i Mohammed   j Ignacio

---

Speak up!

3 🔊 18 Imagine you are speaking on the phone. Listen to these five people. Use the expressions in Exercise 1 to make sure you understand.

Example:
You hear: a
           Can you say that I
           called? My name's
           Shuang Liang.
You say: Sorry. How do you spell
           that?

a spell?
b didn't catch that
c repeat?
d spell?
e more slowly?

Learning tip

Don't worry if you can't understand every word. Accept that you may sometimes need to ask someone to repeat or explain what they mean. The most important thing is that you must tell someone when you don't understand.

C Listening – Taking messages

1 🔊**21** Geena is listening to her voicemail messages on her mobile phone. Listen and match each message (a–c) with a reason for the call (1–3).

Message a ⎯⎯⎯⎯⎯⎯   1 prices for a new project
Message b ⎯⎯⎯⎯⎯⎯   2 questions about a contract
Message c   3 information about the
                          Shelford project

2 🔊**21** Listen again and complete Geena's notes.

> *David Brown*
> *wants to meet on* ....**Friday**.......... *at* ....*pm*
> *Call 02*...................................
>
> *Susan from* ....
> *can't find my* .... *report (needs it before 4pm)*
> *Call asap. Extension* ....
>
> *Robert* .... *from Shell International*
> *Office: 01*................................... *(before* ....*pm)*
> *Mobile: 07*................................... *(after* ....*pm)*

Sound smart
Saying telephone numbers

1 🔊**22** To say a telephone number in English, say each number separately and put the numbers into groups. Listen to these examples:
  a (UK) 020-7834-5633 =
    oh two oh   seven eight three four   five six double three
  b (US) 212-490-3021 =
    two one two   four nine zero   three zero two one

2 🔊**22** Listen and write the telephone numbers c–g.
  c <u>020 8934 0251</u> ....
  d ....
  e ....
  f ....
  g ....

3 🔊**22** Now say the telephone numbers h–l. Then listen and check
  h 020-7344-1920
  i 02-2964-4930
  j 512-034-763
  k 011-336-5621
  l 07978-462-0988

4 Now practise saying *your* telephone number.

x and Study

D Speaking – Leaving messages

Speaking strategy: Leaving a voicemail message

1 You can use the expressions in **bold** when you leave a voicemail message. Match two expressions (a–j) with each explanation (1–5).

a Hello. **This is** Lisa.
b **I'm phoning to** tell you about …
c Thanks a lot. **Bye**.
d **My mobile number is** …
e Hello. **My name's** Lisa Jetson.
f **Could you** send me a brochure, **please**?
g **You can call me on** …
h **I'm calling to** ask about …
i Talk to you later. **Bye for now.**
j **Please** ring me back this afternoon.

1 giving your name ..a, e..
2 giving the reason for your call ....
3 asking someone to do something ....
4 giving your contact details ....
5 finishing the call ....

Speak up!

2 (•123) **Listen to four voicemail announcements and use the ideas below to leave messages. Use your own name.**

Example:
You hear: a
        This is the voicemail for Peter Bradshaw. Please leave a message.
You say: Hello. This is (your name). I'm phoning to tell you the contract is
        ready. Please call me back. You can call me on 3895613.

a the contract is ready / call me back / 3895613
b we need to arrange a meeting / ring me back / 0465-013-645
c want to ask about your prices / send me a brochure / 45 Green Street, Manchester, MN1 6TR
d I've finished the report / call me on cell phone / 07960 235648

Class bonus

1 Phone three classmates and leave a message on their mobile phone, in English! Give your name and the reason for your call. Say what action is necessary. Give your contact details and then finish the call.
2 Listen to any messages on your mobile phone. Take notes, and call back giving your reply

E X tra practice

Find a friend who wants to practise their English. Agree to send each other a message in English every day!

Can-do checklist

Tick what you can do.

	Can do	Need more practice
I can make and receive telephone calls.		
I can take and leave messages.		
I can spell names and addresses, and say telephone numbers.		
I can leave voicemail messages.		

Unit 14
Are there any questions?

Get ready to listen and speak

○ Have you ever been to a talk or presentation in English?

○ Did you enjoy it? How much did you understand?
75%+ ☐   about 50% ☐   less than 30% ☐

○ Number these parts of a presentation in the correct order (1–5).
_____ Questions and answers
_____ Main section
_____ Introduction
__1_ Welcome
_____ Conclusion

go to Useful language p. 83

A Listening – Beginning a presentation

1 🔊 24 **Listen to three speakers begin their talk. Match each speaker with the expression (a–c) they use to welcome the audience.**

a George   1 Good morning, everyone.
b Amy   2 Hello everyone, and welcome.
c Ben   3 Hello. It's great to see you all here today.

2 🔊 24 **Listen again. Write the topic of each presentation.**

a George _new website_ _____
b Amy _____
c Ben _____

3 **How does each speaker introduce their topic?**
🔊 24 **Listen again and complete the expression each speaker uses.**

a George: The ____purpose____ of this talk is to …
b Amy: In this _____ I want to …
c Ben: Today I'm going to _____ to you about …

Ben

Did you know …?

Using visual aids effectively is an important part of any presentation. When you give a presentation, make sure that slides, charts, or graphs are clear and well-presented. This will help your audience understand the most important points you want to make.

B Listening – Giving an outline

1 🔊 **25** **Listen to Ben give an outline of his talk. Number each section of Ben's talk in order (1–4).**

...... show you how to order.

..1.. talk about the new computer program.

...... tell you how to contact us.

...... explain how to search for a product.

2 🔊 **25** **Look at the signposts in bold. Listen to Ben's outline again and tick ✓ the signposts you hear.**

To start with I'll talk about ☑
First, I'll show you ☐
I'll begin by looking at ☐
Then I'll explain ☐
Next we'll consider ☐
After that I'll show you ☐
Finally I'll tell you ☐

Learning tip

When you are listening to a presentation, listen for the words the speaker stresses. These are often the important words. Also notice how the speaker moves their voice up and down. This will help you to understand.

Did you know ...?

Signposts are words and expressions we use to show the order of a presentation.

Sound smart
Stress on important words

1 🔊 **25** Speakers often put more stress on the important words, to help the audience understand. Listen to Ben again. Notice how the important words have more stress.

To <u>start</u> with I'll <u>talk</u> about the new <u>computer</u> <u>program</u> we are <u>using</u>. <u>Then</u> I'll <u>explain</u> how to <u>search</u> for a <u>product</u>.

2 🔊 **25** Now read this part of Ben's presentation. Underline the words you think are important, and should have more stress. Then listen and check.

After that I'll show you how to order, and finally I'll tell you how to contact us if you have a problem.

3 Imagine you are giving this presentation and read both parts aloud. Put more stress on the important words.

C Listening – Main section

1 🔊 **26** **Ben is explaining the company's new ordering system. Listen and write the signposts he uses to introduce each point (a–d).**

a .... First .... b ....
c .... d ....

2 🔊 **26** **Listen again and complete the notes on the right.**

Using the new ordering system

a type in the customer's .... name ....
and ....

b choose the .... the
customer wants to ....

c select the .... the customer
wants

d enter your ....

D Listening – Conclusion

1 🔊 **27 Listen to Ben's conclusion and write true (T) or false (F) next to the statements below.**

a They started developing the new system last year. ..F..
b The new system is ready now. ......
c With the new system, there will be no mistakes. ......
d The new system will be cheaper. ......

2 🔊 **27 Listen again and complete the expressions Ben uses in his conclusion.**

To summarize the main points
In _____
To thank the audience
Thanks for _____

3 🔊 **28 Listen to Amy conclude her presentation. Complete the expressions she uses.**

To summarize the main points
To_____
To thank the audience
Thank you _____ for _____

Er…to sum up, then...

E Listening – Questions and answers

1 🔊 **29 Listen to Ben respond to some questions. Does he agree or disagree with each question? Tick ✓ your answers.**

	Agrees	Disagrees
a	☐	✓
b	☐	☐
c	☐	☐
d	☐	☐
e	☐	☐
f	☐	☐

2 🔊 **29 Listen again and complete each expression Ben uses to agree or disagree.**

a Hmm. I'm ____not sure____ I agree.
b That's a very _____ .
c I _____ that's exactly right.
d I couldn't _____ more.
e I think you may be _____ about that.
f I think you're _____ .

Class bonus

Prepare a one-minute presentation on a topic that you like. You should have an introduction, outline, main section and conclusion. Use the language in this unit to help you. Practise your presentation, remembering to stress the important words. When you are ready, give your presentation to the class.

F Speaking – Talking about the presentation

Speaking strategy: Saying what you think

1 Match each expression in **bold** (a–e) with a function (1–2).

a **I think** it was interesting. __2__
b **What did you think of** the presentation? ......
c **Did you enjoy** the talk? ......
d **I really enjoyed** it. ......
e **I didn't enjoy** it very much. ......

1 to ask for someone's opinion
2 to give your own opinion

Speak up!

2 **30** Anna and James are coming out from a presentation. Number each line of this conversation in order (1–5). Listen and check.

...... Oh dear. Why do you think that?
...... I liked it. I think it was very interesting.
__1__ What did you think of the presentation?
...... Really? I don't agree. I think it was a bit boring.
...... Because there was nothing new in it.

3 **30** Listen again. Pause the recording and speak Anna's words. Then listen again and speak James' words.

4 **31** Imagine you are coming out of a presentation. Listen to the questions and use the ideas below to answer. Use the expressions in **Focus on ...** to help you.

Example:
You hear: a
        Did you enjoy the talk?
You say: Yes, I think it was very good.

a ☺   b ☺   c ☺   d ☹   e ☺   f ☹

Focus on ...
giving opinions

Write each expression in the correct place.

| very interesting | all right | OK | a bit boring |
| not that good | really good | | |

☹	☺	☺
----------------------	----------------------	*very interesting*
----------------------	----------------------	----------------------

E**X**tra practice

Phone your nearest British Council office and ask about their programme of cultural talks and events about the UK. Go to one that interests you, and take a friend.

Can-do checklist

Tick what you can do.

	Can do	Need more practice
I can understand the organization of a presentation or talk.		
I can recognize signposts that speakers may use at various stages.		
I can listen for stress on important words to help me understand.		
I can talk about a presentation, giving my point of view.		

- How often do you ask questions in a talk or seminar?
  Almost always ☐
  I sometimes ask questions ☐
  I prefer to listen to other people's questions ☐

- Do you enjoy expressing your opinion?
  Yes, I like to say what I think. ☐
  No. It's difficult for me to discuss my opinions. ☐
  It depends on the topic! ☐

go to Useful language p. 83

Learning tip

Before a seminar, always make notes of any important points you want to make, and any questions you want to ask. Preparing well in this way will help you participate actively in the seminar.

A Listening – In a seminar

1 🎧32 **Philip and Ana are undergraduate students at college. They are taking part in a seminar. Listen and tick ✓ the topic of the seminar.**

crime ......   education ......   sport ......   science ......   politics ......

2 🎧32 **Listen again and tick ✓ True or False for each statement.**

		True	False
a	EFA is a programme run by the United Nations.	✓	☐
b	EFA stands for Education For Anyone.	☐	☐
c	EFA aims to make sure education is free for everyone.	☐	☐
d	The report Ana read is for countries in Africa and Asia.	☐	☐
e	There are 10 million more primary students than 10 years ago.	☐	☐

Did you know ...?

The United Nations estimates there are nearly 80 million children around the world who do not go to school, and around 780 million adults who cannot read and write. It is a goal of the UN to make sure that by 2015 children everywhere can go to primary school.

B Speaking – Asking questions

Speaking strategy: Asking for clarification

1 When you don't understand, you can use these expressions to ask someone to explain.

What do you mean exactly?
Can you explain that, please?
Can you say a bit more about that, please?
Could you go into more detail on that, please?

2 🔊 32 Listen to the extract of the seminar again. Tick ✓ the expression that you hear.

Speak up!

3 🔊 33 Imagine you are in a seminar. Listen to each statement and use the ideas below to ask for clarification.

Example:
You hear: a
        The biggest cause is lack of funding by some governments.
You say: What do you mean exactly?

a mean?
b more detail?
c explain?
d mean?
e say a bit more?

C Listening – Understanding opinions

1 🔊 34 Listen to Teresa, Kate and Sam discuss the future of computers in education. Match each person with their opinion(s).

Sam _b_
Teresa ___
Kate ___

a everyone will learn at home, on a computer
b computers will become more important in education
c computers will one day replace teachers
d children need to learn from each other
e there will always be schools

2 🔊 34 Listen again and complete the expressions for agreeing and disagreeing.

Agreeing
I _____ .

Disagreeing
I don't _____ .
I'm not _____ I agree.

D Speaking – Expressing opinions

Speaking strategy: Agreeing and disagreeing

1 Look at these expressions for agreeing and disagreeing. <u>Underline</u> the strongest.

a I agree.
I think you're right.
I agree completely.

b I don't agree.
I don't agree at all.
I'm not sure I agree.

2 Match each statement (a–f) with a reply (1–6).

a I thought that seminar was excellent.
b All students should wear a school uniform.
c We always have too much homework.
d The new Maths teacher is really good.
e The food is terrible at this school.
f That exam was hard.

1 I don't agree. They should wear what they want.
2 I'm not sure I agree. I thought it was quite easy.
3 I agree completely. I never have any free time.
4 I agree. I really enjoyed it.
5 I think you're right. I'm starting to enjoy maths now!
6 I don't agree at all. I think it's great!

Speak up!

3 (35) Now listen to these statements and use the ideas below to agree ✓ or disagree ✗.

Example:
You hear: a
There are too many exams.
You say: I think you're right.

a ✓   b ✗   c ✓
d ✗   e ✓   f ✗

4 (35) Listen again and use your own opinions to agree or disagree.

E Speaking – Exchanging opinions

Speaking strategy: Asking for and giving opinions

1 Look at the expressions in bold. Match each expression (a–d) with a use (1–2).

a **I think that** all children should go to school.
b **Do you think that** university education should be free?
c **In my opinion** education is really important.
d **Do you agree that** all children should study languages?

1 to give your opinion _a,_
2 to ask for someone's opinion
_____

Speak up!

2 Imagine you are discussing the topic of education. Use the ideas below to ask for someone's opinion.

Example: a
You say: Do you think that the government should spend more on education?

a government / spend more / education?
b education / be free / everyone?
c children / have right to / good education?
d children / learn about / politics / school?
e schools / teach religion?
f poor families / get money / send children to school?

3 (36) Listen. Pause the recording after each question and answer giving your own opinion. Use I think ... and In my opinion.

Example: a
You hear: Do you think that the government should spend more on education?
You say: Yes, in my opinion the government should spend more. / No, in my opinion they shouldn't.

F Listening – Interrupting to make your point

1 🔊37 **Listen to this discussion and complete the expressions you can use to interrupt someone.**

a Sorry, do you _____ if I interrupt?

b Can I say _____ here?

c Sorry, but can I make a _____ ?

2 🔊37 **Listen again and complete these responses.**

a Can you _____ while I finish?

b Sure, go _____

c Yes, of _____

3 Which response in Exercise 2 does *not* allow someone to interrupt? _____

Focus on ...
Me too/Me neither

1 Look at the examples. Underline two expressions you can use to agree.

A: I really enjoy this class.   A: I don't like maths.
B: Me too.   B: Me neither.

2 Which expression do you use ...

a after a positive sentence? _____

b after a negative sentence? _____

3 Write *Me too* or *Me neither* after each statement below to agree.

a I didn't like that seminar. __Me neither.__

b I think that's an interesting idea. _____

c I don't think that's important. _____

d I really enjoyed that class. _____

e I hate exams! _____

f I didn't do very well in that exam. _____

g I really like languages. _____

h I don't enjoy sport. _____

Class bonus

Make a group of three or four. Discuss each statement (a–f) in Exercise 2. Give your opinion and ask your classmates for their opinion. Remember to interrupt, if necessary, when you want to make your point.

E✗tra practice

Turn to pages 98–99 and find recording 34 of the discussion in section C. Underline the language people use to exchange opinions. Listen and notice the way people use their voice to stress important information. Then choose one person and listen again; try to speak at the same time.

Can-do checklist

Tick what you can do.

	Can do	Need more practice
I can ask for clarification, and explain what I mean.		
I can agree and disagree with others.		
I can give my opinion and ask for other people's opinions.		
I can interrupt someone to make a point.		

Get ready to listen and speak

○ When did you start studying English?

○ How often do you study English now?
every day ☐   once or twice a week ☐   when I have time ☐

go to Useful language p. 83

A Listening – Class schedules

Did you know …?

A *semester* in American English is a *term* in British English, and a *vacation* in American English is a *holiday* in British English.

1 🔊38 **Monika and Yuri are students at Westbrook International College. Listen to them talk about their new class schedules. How many classes is Monika taking this term?** _____

2 🔊38 **Listen again and complete Monika's weekly schedule.**

Ⓦ **Westbrook International College**

Weekly schedule   **Monika Wessel**

Class	Time	Day(s)
Culture Studies	8:30am	_____ & Thursdays
_____	10am	Tuesdays & Thursdays
Language Development	_____	_____
_____	9:40am	_____
Communication Studies	_____	_____

Focus on … prepositions

Complete each sentence with *at, in* or *on*.

a I've got Culture Studies ___on___ Tuesdays.

b I have a class _____ Social Change.

c I'll see you _____ eleven _____ Room 351.

d I don't study _____ weekends.

e I don't have any classes _____ night.

f I'm free _____ Friday afternoons.

g I always have classes _____ the morning.

h This class finishes _____ four o'clock.

i My next class starts _____ ten minutes.

B Speaking – Talking about your studies

Speaking strategy: Asking about schedules

1 Write the words in the correct order to complete these expressions.

a start? / When / course / the / does
  When does the course start?

b in? / room / Which / is / it
  ----

c classess / How many / there / are / a week?

  ----

d classes? / When / the / are
  ----

e the / course? / teaching / Who's

Class bonus

Write down your weekly class schedule. Ask and answer questions about your schedule with a partner.

Speak up!

2 🔊39 Imagine you are studying at a language school in England. You want information about next month's course. Listen and use the ideas below to have a conversation with the secretary.

Example:
You hear: a
  Hello. Can I help you?
You say: Yes. When does the next English course start?

a when / next English course / start?
b how many / classes / week?
c when / classes?
d which room?
e who / teaching?

3 Now imagine you are talking to a friend. Use the notes below to tell your friend about the course.

Example: a
You say: The course starts on Monday the fourth of September.

a starts Monday 4th September
b 5 classes week
c Monday-Friday 9-12.
d Room 2A
e teacher: Mr Price

C Listening – Listening to announcements

1 🔊40 Listen to Mrs Havers, the Course Administrator, tell students about some special guest lectures this month. Complete the chart.

2 🔊40 Listen again. Who should go to …

a Dr Grimshaw's lecture?
  all new students

b Mr Collins' lecture?
  ----

c Prof Kaminski's lecture?

Special Lectures this month	Lecture title	Date	Place
Dr Grimshaw	Study Skills	....	....
Mr Collins	....	....	....
Prof Kaminski	....	....	....

Learning tip

After you answer a question it's a good idea to return it by saying *How about you? / What about you?* This helps to keep the conversation going, and shows you are interested.

Unit 16 I'll hand it in tomorrow

D Listening – Understanding instructions

1 (41) **Listen to these teachers give homework assignments. Write the number of each assignment (a–e) next to the correct topic.**

..... The Future of the English Language
..... How to be a successful language learner
_a_ Grammar and pronunciation
..... Language Development
..... Language and Culture

2 (41) **Listen again and complete each assignment.**

3 (41) **Listen once more and write the day or date when students must finish each assignment.**

a _tomorrow afternoon_
b ....
c ....
d ....
e ....

a do some grammar and pronunciation
___exercises___ .
b write a _____ essay.
c read _____ articles.
d prepare a _____ on the future of
the English Language.
e prepare a _____ talk.

E Listening – Making arrangements

(42) **Listen to Mike speak to his supervisor, Dr Gupta. Answer the questions.**

a What assignment can't he do on time?
his mid-term report
b Why can't he meet the deadline? ....
c When will he start work? ....
d What new deadline does Dr Gupta give?
....

Sound smart
Intonation to confirm

1 (43) Listen to this extract from the conversation above. Notice how Mike's voice goes up when he confirms the date.
Dr Gupta: It will take you a bit of time to do all the reading. Well, what about next Friday?
Mike: You mean Friday 27th?

2 (44) Listen and respond to these statements. Repeat the information making your voice go up.
Example:
You hear: a
Please hand this in by Wednesday.
You say: By Wednesday?

74 Work and Study

F Speaking – Overcoming difficulties

Speaking strategy: Apologizing

1 Look at this extract from the conversation between Mike and Dr. Gupta. <u>Underline</u> the expression that Mike uses to apologize.

Mike: I'm sorry, but I don't think I can hand the mid-term report in on time.

Dr Gupta: I see. Why not?

Mike: I've been ill this week and I couldn't do any work.

2 You can also use the expressions in bold to apologize.

I'm very sorry, but I haven't done the homework.
I'm really sorry, but I haven't finished the report yet.
I'm afraid that my assignment will be late.

Speak up!

3 Number each line of the conversation in order (1–6).

...... Yes, what is it?
...... Would Friday be OK?
_1_ Excuse me. Mr Gaffrey?
...... I'm very sorry but I haven't done the report yet.
...... Yes, that's all right. But no later than Friday, please.
...... I see. So when can you hand it in?

4 Imagine you have not finished your homework. Use the ideas below to apologize and ask permission to hand it in late. Use the expressions in Focus on ... to help you.

Example: a
You say: I'm sorry I haven't finished my essay. Could I hand it in on Thursday?

a essay not finished / Thursday?
b project not done / next Friday OK?
c homework not done / tomorrow?
d English project not finished / next week?
e course work not quite finished / tomorrow?

Focus on ...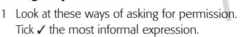
asking for permission

1 Look at these ways of asking for permission. Tick ✓ the most informal expression.
  a Could I hand my essay in tomorrow? ......
  b Would next Friday be OK? ......
  c Can I give it to you next week? ......

2 Write the words in the correct order to make questions asking for permission.
  a hand / report / my / I / Could / in / on / Tuesday
    <u>Could I hand my report in on Tuesday</u> ?
  b OK / Monday / be / Would
    ----
  c I / give / homework / to / you / my / Can / tomorrow

    ?
  d hand / in / project / Could / I / my / week / next

    ?

EX**tra practice**

Make a note of your typical weekly schedule. Then imagine you are telling a friend. Talk about your schedule, and if possible record what you say. Listen to yourself afterwards. Can you identify any areas you could improve (for example, your grammar, pronunciation, etc.)?

Can-do checklist

Tick what you can do.

	Can do	Need more practice
I can ask about and understand schedules (class times, days, etc.).		
I can understand announcements about lectures (where, when, etc.).		
I can understand instructions for homework.		
I can apologize for delays.		

Section 1

🔊 145 **Listen and reply to each statement you hear. Circle your answer.**

1
a Can I take a message?
b How may I help you?
c Yes. Who's calling, please?

2
a Yes, we do.
b Sorry, I'm afraid we don't.
c No, I'm afraid not.

3
a Me neither.
b Me too.
c Yes, I do.

4
a Really? Why not?
b I'm afraid not.
c That's OK.

5
a I agree.
b Me too.
c Yes, they are.

6
a I'm afraid I don't understand.
b Can you speak more slowly, please?
c Could you spell that for me, please?

7
a I'm afraid not.
b Is tomorrow morning OK?
c Yes, that's fine.

8
a Yes, I know.
b Can I help you?
c Thank you very much.

9
a Thanks a lot. Bye.
b That's OK. I'll call back later.
c Can you put me through?

10
a Me too.
b I thought it was great.
c Sure, go ahead.

Section 2

🔊 146 **Read each situation. Then listen and tick ✓ the best answer.**

1 You answer a question and want to ask someone else's opinion. What do you say?
   a ......   b ......   c ......

2 You haven't done your homework and you need to apologize to your teacher. What do you say?
   a ......   b ......   c ......

3 You are in a seminar and want to ask the speaker to clarify something. What do you say?
   a ......   b ......   c ......

4 You arrive at a company and you want to know where the reception is. What do you say?
   a ......   b ......   c ......

5 A visitor to your company is standing at reception. The receptionist is not there. What do you say?
   a ......   b ......   c ......

6 A customer asks for a price list. What do you say?
   a ......   b ......   c ......

7 Your boss, Yolanda, is out of the office. You want to leave a message with her secretary. What do you say?
   a ......   b ......   c ......

8 You want to use the photocopier soon, so you want to ask your colleague not to use it. What do you say?
   a ......   b ......   c ......

9 The office photocopier is broken. You call an office supplies company. What do you say?
   a ......   b ......   c ......

10 Your boss asks you to copy a report. What do you say?
   a ......   b ......   c ......

Section 3

Read each situation and circle your answer.

1 What should you do if you don't understand what someone is saying?
   a Say *Sorry, can you repeat that, please?*
   b Smile to show that you are listening.
   c Try to change the subject.

2 When you make notes of things people ask you to do, should you …
   a write everything in complete sentences?
   b note the important information only?
   c try to remember and email them if you have a question?

3 Which of these expressions tells you a speaker is about to come to the end of their presentation?
   a To give you an example …
   b To sum up, …
   c Next, I'll …

4 What should you say if someone is speaking too quickly?
   a Could you spell that for me?
   b Sorry, but your accent is hard to understand.
   c Can you speak a bit more slowly, please?

5 What can you say to introduce yourself on the telephone?
   a Hello. This is …
   b Hello. I'm …
   c Hello. Here is …

6 When you are listening to a presentation, should you …
   a close your eyes to listen more carefully?
   b try to notice the speaker's body language?
   c take lots of notes to look at later?

7 Which is the best way to say goodbye to a visitor?
   a Bye for now.
   b Have a safe journey.
   c I have to go now.

8 In a seminar, what should you say if you want to interrupt someone?
   a Excuse me, but can I make a point?
   b Sorry, but can I finish what I'm saying?
   c Sorry, I want to say something.

9 What's a good way to pass on a message?
   a Mr Brown wants you to phone him.
   b Phone Mr Brown.
   c You have to phone Mr Brown.

10 Which sentence is most polite?
   a Can you give me a catalogue, please?
   b Could you give me a catalogue, please?
   c Please give me a catalogue.

Section 4

Read each statement and write a possible reply.

1 Could you reduce the price, please?
   ----

2 Can you keep this until next Wednesday?
   ----

3 Do you need any help?
   ----

4 Can you deliver?
   ----

5 This box is really heavy.
   ----

6 What was the talk like?
   ----

7 I thought that meeting was a waste of time.
   ----

8 Do you mind if I interrupt?
   ----

9 I didn't enjoy that class at all.
   ----

10 Can you finish the report by Friday?

Appendix 1
Useful language

This appendix contains a list of expressions which are useful when carrying out the listening and speaking tasks in each unit. The expressions are divided into *Things you can say* and *Things you might hear*. All the expressions are recorded on the Audio CD.

You can use this appendix in the following ways.

Before you begin each unit:
1 Look at the expressions and use your dictionary to check the meaning of any words you do not understand.
2 Look at the expressions, but try to work out the meaning of any words you do not understand *when you see or hear them in the unit*. This is more challenging, but it is a very useful skill to practise.

After you complete each unit:
3 Look at the expressions and check that you understand. Try to think of different examples using the same key words. Find the key words and expressions in the Audioscript to see them in context.
4 Listen to the expressions, and notice the stress and rhythm of the speaker. You may want to mark sentence stress in a highlighter pen. Listen again and repeat each phrase, practising the stress and rhythm.
5 Listen again to the expressions and notice the pronunciation of any difficult words. You may want to mark word stress in a highlighter pen. Listen once more and repeat each word, practising the word stress.
6 Cover a column, then listen to each expression and repeat from memory. This helps to focus your listening.

Unit 1

Things you can say	Things you might hear
Hello. My name's …	What's your name?
Hi. I'm …	Where are you from?
Nice to meet you.	Hi there. How's it going?
I'm very well, thank you. And you?	How are you?
How's work at the moment?	Nice to meet you, too.
Do you live in …?	How are things?
It's a great place.	Where are you from?
It's a beautiful city.	What do you do?
You should visit sometime.	Where do you live?
Do you have any children?	Are you married?
Do you enjoy your job?	Bye for now.
Do you have any plans for the weekend?	See you later.
How about you? / What about you?	It was lovely to see you.
	I hope you have a safe journey.

Unit 2

Things you can say	Things you might hear
I'm just looking.	Do you need any help?
Excuse me. Can you help me, please?	It's in the sale.
How much is this hat?	They're half price.
What size is it?	What size do you want?
How much are those jeans?	Would you like to try it on?
What size are they?	The changing rooms are over there.
Can I try them on?	I'm afraid we don't accept cheques.
Do you have this shirt in medium?	It suits you.
I can't find the price.	It fits you perfectly.
Where can I pay?	The cash desk is over there.
I'll pay by credit card.	How would you like to pay?
OK. I'll take it.	
I think I'll leave it.	

Unit 3

Things you can say	Things you might hear
Do you have a set menu?	Would you like to see the menu?
Can I have the menu, please?	Can I get you anything to drink?
What specials do you have today?	Are you ready to order?
What do you recommend?	What would you like for starter?
I'll have the soup to start with, please.	And for your main course?
Excuse me. What's a Caesar Salad?	How would you like your steak?
What's in the Mexican Mixed Grill?	Who ordered the fish?
Can you tell me what the House Special is, please?	Is everything all right with your meal?
That sounds good.	Would you like a dessert?
How's your chicken?	Can I help you?
What's the soup like?	OK, so that's one double cheeseburger.
It's delicious.	Do you want a regular or large shake?
It's a bit too salty.	Do you want fries with that?
Is service included?	Eat in or take away?
Can I have the bill, please?	

Unit 4

Things you can say	Things you might hear
	I'd like you to meet my husband.
Pleased to meet you.	Please call me Kevin.
Nice to meet you, too.	This is my daughter.
It's a big room with a view of the park.	How was your trip?
Is it OK if I watch TV?	Let me show you to your room.
Do you think I could make a cup of coffee?	On the left is the kitchen.
Would you mind if I invite a friend for dinner?	The dining room is on your right.
Is it OK if I turn up the heating?	The toilet is at the top of the stairs.
	Do you want to unpack?
	There's a pay phone at the end of the street.

Unit 5

Things you can say	Things you might hear
I'd like to open a bank account.	Can you fill in this form?
I need to order a new cheque book.	Please can you write your address on the back?
I'd like to check my balance, please.	We need proof of your identity.
I want to cash this cheque, please.	Can you show me your bank card, please?
I have to send some money abroad.	You'll get a bank statement every month.
Can I have ten first class stamps, please?	I'll weigh it for you.
I'd like to send this parcel by registered mail.	Normal airmail will be $23.
How much is it to send this letter to …?	That'll be €16.
Can I send this by airmail, please?	Is it urgent?
Can I change some dollars, please?	The commission is two per cent.
What's today's exchange rate?	We charge £3.50 commission.
Do you charge commission?	One euro will get you 67 pence.
That's fine.	
I'll think about it.	

Unit 6

Things you can say	Things you might hear
I don't feel very well.	What's the matter?
I've got a stomachache / backache.	Oh, dear. I'm sorry to hear that.
I have earache / toothache.	Poor you! How awful.
I've got a terrible cough / sore throat / cold.	I hope you feel better soon.
I think I have a temperature.	Maybe you should see a doctor.
Have you got something for sunburn?	You shouldn't go to work.
What have you got for a headache?	I think you should go to bed.
How many tablets should I take?	You can try this cream. It's very good.
How much cream should I use?	You can see Doctor Brown at 10.30.
I'd like to make an appointment, please.	I'll give you a prescription for some tablets.
	Take two tablets, twice a day.
	Just stay in bed and take it easy.

Unit 7

Things you can say	Things you might hear
	Can I have your ticket and passport, please?
Yes, of course. Here you are.	How many bags are you checking in?
Here it is. / Here they are.	Did you pack your bags yourself?
Here you are. / Here you go.	Are there any sharp items in your hand luggage?
I'm taking this hand luggage.	Would you like an aisle seat or a window seat?
Where can I get a taxi / hire a car, please?	This is your boarding card.
Where can I find a bureau de change?	Where are you travelling from today?
Where's the bus station, please?	What's the purpose of your visit?
How can I get to the city centre?	Do you have anything to declare?
Can you recommend a good hotel?	Here. I'll take your bag.
Thanks very much for your help.	
I'm exhausted!	

Unit 8

Things you can say	Things you might hear
How much is a single room, please?	A standard single is €60 a night.
I'd like to book a double room.	When would you like to book it for?
Do you have any non-smoking rooms?	I'm afraid we're fully booked.
Are the rooms air-conditioned?	All our rooms are en-suite.
Is breakfast included?	Breakfast is £10 extra.
How far is it to the city centre?	Can I have your name, please?
Do you have a room with a view?	I hope you enjoy your stay.
Do you have internet access?	Here's your room key.
Can I have a wake-up call?	We have a fitness centre on the top floor.
Is room service available?	We have 24-hour room service.
Do you have a laundry service?	
When's the check-out time?	
I'm afraid that the air-conditioning doesn't work.	
Sorry to bother you, but the television doesn't work.	

Unit 9

Things you can say	Things you might hear
Can I have a single to …, please?	The next train's at 3.15.
How long does it take?	The next train leaves at four thirty.
What time's the next train?	There's a bus at 9.45.
How much is it?	The train to Cambridge will depart from Platform 9.
What platform does it leave from?	The 7.50 intercity service to … is delayed.
Excuse me. Where's the bus station, please?	Go along here and turn left.
How do I get to the Art Museum?	The train station's on the right / on the corner.
Can you tell me where the station is, please?	The post office is just past the bank.
Where's the Tourist Office, please?	

Unit 10

Things you can say	Things you might hear
Are there any good markets here?	… is very popular.
What museums do you recommend?	… is famous for markets.
Where's the best place to go shopping?	It's not far from here.
Are there any temples I can visit near here?	There's a guided walk starting soon.
Is there a guided tour I can go on?	A tour bus leaves from just across the road.
What shall we do?	That's fine with me.
How about going to …?	That's a good idea. / That sounds great.
Why don't we go to …?	It's up to you. / I don't mind.
I'd rather not do that today.	
How beautiful! / It's fantastic!	

Unit 11

Things you can say	Things you might hear
Do you need any help?	I'm here to see Mr/Mrs … .
May I help you?	I'm looking for … / I'm trying to find …
Let me show you the way.	Do you have a price list?
I'll give you a new catalogue.	Can you tell me where the sales office is, please?
I'll give you a hand.	What special offers have you got?
I'll do it straight away.	Do you know where [Charles] is?
Susan wants you to call her.	Can you ask him to call me when he gets in?
OK. I'll tell him.	Can you tell him to …?
Sure. No problem.	Can you send an email to …?
It was great to see you again.	Can you call … and ask him to …?
Have a safe journey.	Would you mind emailing … at head office for me?
Thanks very much for coming.	Please can you make six copies?

Unit 12

Things you can say	Things you might hear
Do you sell …?	No, I'm afraid we don't.
I'm looking for …	Yes, we do. We sell all the main brands.
Do you repair computers?	No, I'm afraid we don't do repairs.
Can you send someone to repair it?	We have a wide range of …
Can you find out the price, please?	We can send someone this afternoon.
The price is a bit high.	That's the best price we can offer you.
Can you give me a discount?	The next delivery will go out on Friday.
Do you charge for delivery?	We deliver free of charge.
When can you deliver?	Do you have an account with us?
It's very urgent.	Is that everything?
Could you send it by special delivery, please?	I'll keep it until 5pm on Wednesday.
Can you tell me when the order is ready?	
I think this one is better/lighter/cheaper.	

Unit 13

Things you can say	Things you might hear
Can I have extension 726, please?	Who's calling please?
Can I speak to …, please?	I'll put you through.
Can you ask him to call me back when he's free?	Sorry, the line's busy at the moment.
Can you say that I called?	Would you like to leave a message?
Can I leave a message?	Can you hold the line, please?
Can you put me through?	Could you call back later?
I'm afraid I didn't quite catch that.	He's on another call right now.
Can you repeat that, please?	I'm afraid he's out of the office at the moment.
How do you spell that?	Hello. Lisa speaking.
Can you speak a little more slowly, please?	This is George here.
Please call me as soon as you get this message.	You can reach me on my mobile.

Unit 14

Things you can say	Things you might hear
I really enjoyed that presentation. What did you think of the presentation? Did you enjoy the talk? I think that it was very interesting. I didn't enjoy it very much. Why do you think that? It was a bit boring. Really? I don't agree.	Hello everyone, and welcome. The purpose of this talk is to … Today I'm going to talk to you about … To start with I'll talk about … I'll begin by talking about … After that I'll … / Then I'll … / Finally, I'll … A good example of this is … To give you another example, … So, in conclusion … / To sum up … Would anyone like to ask a question? I couldn't agree more. I think you may be wrong about that.

Unit 15

Things you can say	Things you might hear
Do you agree that …? I think you're right. I agree completely. I'm not sure I agree. I don't agree at all. What do you mean exactly? Can you explain that? Can I say something here? Sorry. Do you mind if I interrupt?	What do you think of …? Do you think that …? I think you're right. That's a good point. Can you say a bit more about that? That's a good point. Can you wait a moment while I finish? Sure. Go ahead. I'd like to ask you about …

Unit 16

Things you can say	Things you might hear
Have you got your schedule for this term? When does the next course start? Which room is it in? How many classes are there a week? When are the classes? Who's teaching the course? Do you have the afternoon free? What other classes do you have? I'm very sorry but I haven't done the homework. I don't think I can hand the report in on time.	I want to tell you about some special lectures this month. I recommend that all new students attend this lecture. That should be a very interesting talk. For homework I want you to … Give it to me first thing on Monday morning. Please do this in time for the seminar. Please hand this in by Wednesday. The deadline for this is Monday 21st. Do you think you can finish it by the end of next week? When can you hand it in?

Appendix 2
Pronunciation features

Sound smart

Sound smart gives additional guidance to help you develop your pronunciation skills. You will find a *Sound smart* in most units of this book. This appendix contains a list of the pronunciation areas covered in *Sound smart* at this level.

You can use this appendix in the following ways:
1 Choose a pronunciation focus you want to practise. Go to the unit where the *Sound smart* section appears and practise again.
2 Find a pronunciation focus that you think is especially useful. Practise once more, but this time record yourself and listen afterwards. Try to identify areas you can improve.
3 Practise again, but this time listen to a different recording. Look in the Audioscript first to find a suitable recording.

Practise each pronunciation focus in *Sound smart* several times. The more you practise, the better your pronunciation will become.

Unit 1	Intonation to show interest
Unit 2	Sentence stress
Unit 3	Intonation in questions
Unit 4	Linking words together
Unit 5	–
Unit 6	The schwa
Unit 7	–
Unit 8	The schwa /jə/ /djə/
Unit 9	Intonation
Unit 10	Using stress to respond to suggestions
Unit 11	–
Unit 12	Emphasizing alternatives
Unit 13	Spelling names Saying telephone numbers
Unit 14	Stress on important words
Unit 15	–
Unit 16	Intonation to confirm

Appendix 3
Speaking strategies

Speaking strategies are useful techniques to help you communicate in a wide variety of situations. You will find *Speaking strategies* in each unit of this book. This appendix contains a list of the *Speaking strategies* covered at this level.

You can use this appendix in the following ways:

1 Choose a strategy you want to practise. Go to the unit where the strategy appears and practise again.
2 Find a strategy that you think is especially useful. Practise once more, but this time record yourself and listen afterwards. Try to identify areas you can improve. If possible, practise with an English-speaking friend.

Practise each strategy several times. The more you practise, the easier it will be to use the strategies when you need them in real life.

Unit 1	Starting a conversation Responding to information
Unit 2	Showing you understand Asking a shop assistant for help
Unit 3	Asking about dishes on a menu Asking for and expressing opinions Saying you don't understand
Unit 4	Meeting people for the first time Asking for permission Expressing opinions
Unit 5	Explaining what you want Asking about services Accepting or declining a service
Unit 6	Showing sympathy Giving advice Asking about medication Checking important details
Unit 7	Responding to requests Giving clear answers Asking for information
Unit 8	Confirming details Making a complaint
Unit 9	Buying a ticket Asking for and giving directions
Unit 10	Making and responding to suggestions Reacting to what you see Describing places you know

Unit 11	Offering help Passing on messages Asking someone not to do something Saying goodbye to visitors
Unit 12	Making requests Responding to requests Making comparisons
Unit 13	Making sure you understand Leaving a voicemail message
Unit 14	Saying what you think
Unit 15	Asking for clarification Agreeing and disagreeing Asking for and giving opinions
Unit 16	Asking about schedules Apologizing

Appendix 4
Learning tips

Learning tips give additional guidance to help you develop your listening and speaking skills. You will find at least one *Learning tip* in each unit of this book. This appendix contains all the *Learning tip*s from the book. Most *Learning tips* are useful in a wide variety of situations.

You can use this appendix in the following ways:

1 Read each tip carefully and make sure you understand. Go to the unit where the tip appears and practise again.
2 Find a tip for improving your listening. Choose one that you think is especially useful. Practise again, but this time listen to a different recording. Look in the Audioscript first to find a suitable recording.
3 Find a tip for improving your speaking. Choose one you like and practise again, on your own. Record yourself and listen afterwards to identify areas you can improve. If possible, practise with an English-speaking friend.
4 Practise the tips whenever and wherever possible. For example, make a habit of listening to the radio in English, or find a TV programme in English to watch regularly. Try to practise a different tip each time.
5 Use any additional help. For example, turn on the subtitle feature if available when watching a TV programme in English. Some radio stations have audioscripts of their programmes on the Internet. When you listen to songs in English, read the lyrics. If you watch a movie in English on DVD, use the subtitle feature to help you understand.

Take as many opportunities as you can to practise listening and speaking English and you will continue to improve.

Unit 1

Learning tip

Remember to smile, and keep good eye contact when you are speaking to someone. This shows you are interested.

Unit 2

Learning tip

Before you listen, always read the questions and make sure you know what information you are listening for (e.g. a date, a name, a price, etc.).

Unit 3

Learning tip

If possible, prepare yourself *before* you listen or speak in English. Think of the language that you might hear, and what you might need to say.

Learning tip

In a fast food restaurant, look at the pictures around you and the words on the menu board like *large*, *regular* and *small*.

Unit 4

Learning tip

In English, people say *please* and *thank you* a lot. Always say *please* when you ask for permission, and remember to say *thank you*.

Unit 5

Learning tip

Listen for key words to help you identify each place. For example, if you hear *stamps*, then it must be a post office!

Unit 6

Learning tip

Focus your listening. Listen only for the information you need. For example, listen for days, times, and names.

Unit 7

Learning tip

It is sometimes possible to guess what someone is going to say *before* they say it – especially in situations where people use the same language every time (e.g. checking in at an airport or hotel).

Unit8

Learning tip

When you speak in English, don't worry about making mistakes. Keep talking! Don't stop to think or try to translate what to say in your head.

Unit9

Learning tip

Try to *think* in English as much as possible. Whenever you have some free time, think of what you can say in different situations. For example, imagine a tourist stops you in the street and asks you a question. What could they ask? How could you answer?

Unit10

Learning tip

If possible, record yourself speaking. Then listen and think about things you can improve. Is your pronunciation clear? Can you hear any errors?

Unit11

Learning tip

When you listen and take a message, only note the important information. You don't need to write in complete sentences. Keep it short, and try to use abbreviations.

Unit12

Learning tip

When you make a phone call to ask for something, make sure you have all the information you need. Keep the conversation short and say only what you need to say.

Unit13

Learning tip

Don't worry if you can't understand every word. Accept that you may sometimes need to ask someone to repeat or explain what they mean. The most important thing is that you must tell someone when you don't understand.

Unit14

Learning tip

When you are listening to a presentation, listen for the words the speaker stresses. These are often the important words. Also notice how the speaker moves their voice up and down. This will help you to understand.

Unit15

Learning tip

Before a seminar, always make notes of any important points you want to make, and any questions you want to ask. Preparing well in this way will help you participate actively in the seminar.

Unit16

Learning tip

After you answer a question it's a good idea to return it by saying *How about you? / What about you?* This helps to keep the conversation going, and shows you are interested.

Appendix5
Presentation evaluation

This appendix contains an evaluation form for assessing presentations, and a separate form for recording feedback on your own performance. You can photocopy these forms and use them in the following ways:

For self-study

Listen to a talk or presentation on the radio, or television. Consider each question on the *Presentation evaluation* form and give the speaker a grade. Note any areas you think are especially good, or weak, and give a final grade for your overall impression. Ask yourself how the speaker could improve.

In class

Listening to a presentation:
While you listen to a classmate give a presentation, consider each question on the *Presentation evaluation* form and give a grade. Give a final grade for your overall impression, and note any areas you think are especially good, or that need attention. Then tell your classmate your opinion, and add some suggestions to help them improve.

Giving a presentation:
After you have given a presentation, listen to your classmates' opinions of your performance and make a note of their grades on the My performance form. Note any strengths and weaknesses, and listen carefully to any suggestions for improvement. Study the feedback and try to improve on any areas of weakness.

Presentation evaluation

1 = excellent   2 = good   3 = satisfactory   4 = weak

		1	2	3	4
1	Was the talk well-organised?	☐	☐	☐	☐
2	Was the speaker's English accurate?	☐	☐	☐	☐
3	Was the speaker's voice clear and easy to understand?	☐	☐	☐	☐
4	Were any visual aids well-presented and useful?	☐	☐	☐	☐
5	Did the speaker maintain good eye contact?	☐	☐	☐	☐
6	What was your overall impression?	☐	☐	☐	☐

Good points: ....
Weak points: ....

Suggestions for improvement: ....
....

My performance

		Group's grades	Group's comments
1	Organisation		
2	Language		
3	Pronunciation		
4	Use of visual aids		
5	Eye contact		
6	Overall impression		

My strengths: ....
My weaknesses: ....

Group's suggestions for improvement: ....
....

Audioscript

These recordings are mostly in standard British English. Where a speaker has a different accent, it is noted in brackets.

 CD1 Social and Travel

Unit 1

2 (Vladimir = Russian; Yoko = Japanese; Helen and Dan = American)

a Jake: Hi. I'm Jake.
Samantha: Hi, Jake. I'm Samantha. Nice to meet you.
Jake: Nice to meet you too. Are you a friend of Tim's?
Samantha: Yes, I am. We go to college together.

b Vladimir: Hello. My name is Vladimir Petrov.
Yoko: Hello. Pleased to meet you. My name's Yoko Shirai.
Vladimir: Pleased to meet you too.

c Hi. I'm Helen.
Hi. I'm Dan.

d My name's Jake Ward. Nice to meet you.
Nice to meet you, too. My name's Yoko Shirai.

e Hello. My name is Vladimir Petrov.
I'm Helen Richards. Pleased to meet you.
Pleased to meet you too.

f Hello there. I'm Jake. What's your name?
I'm Helen.
Nice to meet you, Helen.

g Hi, I'm Samantha.
Hi Samantha. I'm Vladimir.

3 (Daniela = Italian; Joshua = Canadian; Shizuka = Japanese)

Tom: So, Daniela. Where are you from?
Daniela: I'm from Italy.
Tom: Great. What do you do there?
Daniela: I'm a nurse.
Tom: Really? And where do you live?
Daniela: In Rome. It's the capital.

Tom: Nice to meet you Joshua. So, where are you from?
Joshua: I'm from Canada.
Tom: Oh yes? What do you do there?
Joshua: I'm a sales manager for a small computer company.
Tom: I see. And where do you live?
Joshua: In Vancouver. It's a great place. You should visit sometime.

Tom: Hello Shizuka. Are you from Thailand?
Shizuka: No, actually I'm from Japan.
Tom: Oh, sorry. Japan. What do you do there?
Shizuka: I'm a teacher. I teach science.
Tom: That's great. So do you live in Tokyo?
Shizuka: Yes, that's right.

4
a So you work with computers?
b What do you do?
c I'm a science teacher in a high school.
d Do you live in Manchester?
e I've never been to Portugal.
f So you've got two sisters and one brother?
g You're getting married next month!

5 (Teresa = Brazilian; Ang = Chinese)
Teresa: It's a bit cold today, isn't it?
Ang: Yes, it is. I hope it gets better soon. I want to start playing golf.
Teresa: Oh, really? You play golf? Me too. Who is your favourite player?
Ang: Tiger Woods, for sure.
Teresa: Where do you play?
Ang: Near my home in Shanghai, there's a golf course.
Teresa: So, you live in Shanghai. That's interesting. It's an exciting place, isn't it?
Ang: Yes. There's so much happening there these days. It's amazing. What about you? Where are you from?
Teresa: I'm from Brazil. I live in Brasília, the capital.
Ang: Oh yes. I've never went there.*
Teresa: You should go. It's a beautiful city.

☞ *Did you notice?
Ang says *I've never went there.* A native speaker would say *I've never been there.* [In American English, *I never went there* is also possible.]

6
a Where are you from?
b What do you do?
c Are you married?
d Do you have any children?
e Do you enjoy your job?
f Do you have any plans for the weekend?

7
a I'm from Manchester.
b I'm going on holiday next week.

c I'm starting a new job on Monday.
d I like sport.
e I'm going to a football match tonight.
f My brother lives in New Zealand.

Unit 2

8 (Carlos = Spanish)
Assistant: Excuse me. Do you need any help?
Carlos: No thank you. I am fine. I'm just looking.
Assistant: That shirt's in the sale. Today's the last day.
Carlos: Oh, right. Hmm. Well, I like the colour.
Assistant: It's £20 in the sale. The normal price is forty.
Carlos: Oh, OK. That's quite good. Oh, that jacket is nice. How much is it?
Assistant: That's half price too – £120. It's leather, made in Italy. Would you like to try it on?
Carlos: Oh, yes. I like it a lot. It is too good.*
Assistant: Mmm, yes. I think it suits you.
Carlos: Really? Well, OK then. I'll take it.
Assistant: And the shirt as well?
Carlos: Er. Well, what size it is?*
Assistant: It's a medium. I'm sure it'll fit you, and it will go very nicely with the jacket.
Carlos: OK. I will take the shirt as well!

☞ *Did you notice?
Carlos says *It is too good.* A native speaker would say *It is really good.* He also says *Well, what size it is?* A native speaker would say *What size is it?*

9
a No, I'm sorry. We haven't got this T-shirt in medium.
b Yes, here you are. We've got your size.
c We've got this jacket in brown, but not in black.
d I'm afraid we haven't got it in blue, but we've got it in green.
e These jeans are in the sale. They're half price.
f Yes. You're in luck. This is the last pair we've got, and they're in your size.

🔊 10

a Do you need any help?
b That jacket's in the sale.
c What size do you want?
d Thank you, I'll take it.
e How much is this hat?
f Are these shoes in the sale?
g Where's the cash desk?
h Can I pay by cheque?
i Do you have this shirt in medium?
j Where are the changing rooms, please?

🔊 11 (Kumiko = Japanese)

Kumiko: Excuse me. How much is that coat?
Stallholder: It's a hundred and twenty quid. Do you want to try it on?
Kumiko: Oh, er … yes please.
Stallholder: Here you are.
Kumiko: Thanks. Hmm.
Stallholder: It suits you. You look great.
Kumiko: Thank you.
Stallholder: That's 100% pure wool. From one of the top designers in Paris.
Kumiko: Oh, right. It's very nice, but it's a little expensive.
Stallholder: No it's not! It's a bargain. The normal price for that in the shops is three hundred quid.
Kumiko: Oh, OK. But I think maybe it's too big for me.
Stallholder: It fits you perfectly. Don't worry. Look, you can have it for a hundred. That's a special offer, only for you.
Kumiko: Hmm. £100. OK. I take it!* Can I pay by credit card?
Stallholder: Sorry, dear. Cash only.

☞*Did you notice?

Notice Kumiko says *I take it!* A native speaker would say *I'll take it.*

🔊 12 (b, f = American)

a thirteen pounds
b forty dollars
c fifty euros
d sixteen pounds
e seventy euros
f eighteen dollars

🔊 13 (b = American; d = Australian)

a All the T-shirts on this rack are three pounds ninety-nine.
b Those jeans are in the sale. They're nineteen dollars ninety.
c No, this jacket isn't in the sale, I'm afraid. It's a hundred and eighty-nine euros.

d A: Is this shirt in the sale?
   B: That shirt? Let me just find the price for you. Yes, it's seventeen dollars and fifty cents.
e Let me have a look. Yes, these shoes are twenty-nine pounds ninety-five.
f That black jumper? It's nineteen euros.

🔊 14

Customer: Excuse me. Can you help me, please?
Assistant: Yes, of course. How can I help?
Customer: How much are these trousers? I can't find the price.
Assistant: Er, let me have a look. Here it is. They're £35.
Customer: Oh, OK. Can I try them on?
Assistant: Yes, of course. The changing rooms are over there.

Unit3

🔊 15

a Would you like to see the dessert menu?
b Can I have the bill, please?
c How would you like your steak?
d Are you ready to order?
e Excuse me? Can I have two coffees and a tea, please?
f Is everything all right with your meal?
g Could I have some more rice, please?
h I'll have the soup to start with, please.
i Can you tell me what the House Special is, please?

🔊 16

a Can I get you anything to drink?
b Are you ready to order?
c What would you like for a starter?
d And for your main course?
e Would you like a dessert?

🔊 17

a Do you want dessert?
b Can I take your coat?
c Where do you want to sit?
d What would you like as a starter?

🔊 18

a Could I have a menu, please?
b What do you recommend?
c Do you have a set menu?
d What soft drinks do you have?
e Can I have the bill, please?
f Is service included?
g What specials do you have today?
h Where's the toilet, please?

🔊 19 (speakers a and c = American)

a Mmm. It's excellent. This meat's very tender, and these carrots and peas are really tasty.
b Well, it's not very good, I'm afraid. It's a bit too salty. I can't really taste the tomato.
c The chicken's a bit too spicy for me. I like hot food but this is too hot. The rice is good, though. Waiter! Can I have a glass of water, please?
d It's delicious, and the fruit's all really fresh. Mmm. The pineapple's a bit too sweet for me, though.

🔊 20

a What's your soup like?
b How's your chicken?
c What's the chocolate cake like?
d Is your pizza nice?
e How's the ice-cream?

🔊 21 (Customer = Russian; Assistant = American)

Customer: Oh, hello. Can I have a double cheeseburger, please?
Assistant: Do you want fries with that?
Customer: Erm, yes please.
Assistant: What size?
Customer: Sorry, what do you mean?
Assistant: Do you want small, medium or large fries?
Customer: Oh, er medium, thanks. Sorry, I don't speak well English.*
Assistant: And a drink?
Customer: Erm, yes. A coffee. Small.
Assistant: OK, so that's one double cheeseburger with medium fries and a small coffee. Is that everything?
Customer: Yes, thank you.
Assistant: That's $4.98.

☞*Did you notice?

The Russian man says *I don't speak well English.* This should be *I don't speak English well.*

Unit4

🔊 22

a Mr Jacobs: Now, I'd like you to meet my wife, Carol.
b Mrs Jacobs: Hello. Nice to meet you.
   Mr Jacobs: And this is my daughter, Lisa.
   Lisa: Hi. Nice to meet you.
c Lisa: How was your trip?
d Mr Jacobs: And over here is my son Martin. Martin? Come and say hello.

Martin: Hi there. Pleased to meet you.

Mr Jacobs: Now, let me show you to your room.

23

OK, so let me show you around. This is the hall, of course. On the left is the kitchen … and on the right is the dining room. And then along here, if you follow me, on the right is the lounge. This is where we spend most of our time. OK, so that's the downstairs. Oh, I nearly forgot, there's a toilet here just at the bottom of the stairs. So, let's go upstairs now … On the left is our room, that's my husband Kevin and me. And opposite is Abigail's room. This is your room, along here next to Abigail's. It's quite big. Oh, yes, and the bathroom is at the end. Right, I think that's everything … Do you want to unpack?

24

a The kitchen is downstairs, on the left.
b The dining room is downstairs, on the right.
c The lounge is next to the kitchen.
d The toilet is at the top of the stairs.
e Mr and Mrs Woods' room is at the top of the stairs, on the left
f Abigail's room is next to her parents' room.
g The bathroom is at the end.
h Paula's room is next to the bathroom.

25

a This is the dining room and on the right is the lounge.
b The kitchen is on the left.
c My room is on the right.
d It's a big room with a view of the park.
e Teresa picked up the bag and took it upstairs.
f We left our coats in the kitchen.
g I'd like a cup of tea, please.

26

OK, so breakfast is from 7.30. Anytime is OK. You can have cereal and toast, and make yourself a cup of tea. We always have dinner at 6.30, though, so please don't be late. We don't have a bath, but you can have a shower every morning. The bathroom is busy, so please go in at seven and try to finish by twenty past. I won't clean your room, so you have to keep your room tidy, but I'll wash your towels and sheets once a week. You'll have clothes to wash, so you can do your washing on Sundays. You don't have to do it yourself. I can do it, but it's an extra €10 a week. Er, let me see. What else? Oh, you can use the phone for local calls but

not for international calls, OK? There's a pay phone at the end of the street. You can use that to phone home. Oh, and here's your key. You can keep it with you while you're here, but please come back home before midnight. We like to sleep well in this house! OK, I think that's everything. You can always ask if you're not sure …

Unit5

27

a Can I have ten first class stamps, please?
b I'd like to open a bank account.
c How much is it to send this letter to Mexico?
d I need to order a new cheque book.
e I'd like to check my balance, please.
f I'd like to send this parcel by registered mail.
g I'd like to send this letter special delivery, please.

28 (Bank clerk = Canadian)

We need proof of your identity, so that means your passport, of course, and one other form of ID such as your driving licence … or, if you have one, an ID card is fine. We also need proof of where you live, so something official with your name and address on … a telephone or electricity bill, for example, or if you rent, then your rental contract showing your name and address. Oh, also, if you are a student we need a letter from your school, or, if you have a job, then a letter from your employer.

29 (Bank clerk = Canadian)

Well, this is a basic bank account, so you will get a cash card to use when you want to withdraw money. You can deposit money, too, of course … that's cash and cheques, free, but you can't have a cheque book or a credit card, I'm afraid, with this account, and there's no loan facility.

30

a Customer: I'd like to open an account.
   Clerk: Certainly. Can you fill in this form? Our New Accounts Manager will see you shortly.
b Customer: I want to cash this cheque, please.
   Clerk: Please can you write your address on the back?
c Customer: I need to transfer some money to my savings account.
   Clerk: No problem. Can you show me your bank card, please?

31

a Customer: Oh, er, hello. Er. Yes. Can I send this by airmail, please?
   Clerk: One postcard? Where do you want to send it?
   Customer: To France. Oh, I have three actually.
   Clerk: Three postcards will be £1.50.
   Customer: OK. Thanks.

b (Customer = Russian)
   Customer: How much is it to send this parcel by airmail?
   Clerk: Where's it going to?
   Customer: To Poland?
   Clerk: How much does it weigh?
   Customer: Sorry, I not know.*
   Clerk: If you give it to me, please, I'll weigh it for you.
   Customer: Oh, yes. Thank you.
   Clerk: Let me see … er, normal airmail will be £11.70.
   Customer: OK. Thanks.

☞ *Did you notice?
The Russian man says *I not know*. A native speaker would say *I don't know*.

c Customer: Can I send this letter by airmail, please?
   Clerk: Of course. Where's it going to?
   Customer: To Japan. How much is it please?
   Clerk: That's £3.
   Customer: Ok, thanks. How long will it take?
   Clerk: About five days.
   Customer: Ok. Thanks a lot.

d (Customer = Australian)
   Customer: Hello. I'd like to send this letter to Australia, please. It's quite urgent.
   Clerk: OK. If it's urgent, you should probably send it by special delivery.
   Customer: How much will that cost?
   Clerk: That'll be £6.
   Customer: Thanks a lot.

32

a How can I help you?
b Is it urgent?
c Well, you'll probably want to send it by surface mail, then.
d By surface mail? Usually four to six weeks.
e Let me see. It weighs 1.4 kilos, so that will be £21 by airmail and £10.20 as a surface parcel.
f Usually six to ten days.

33

a Clerk: The commission is 2 per cent.
   Customer: That's fine. Can I change some dollars please?
b Clerk: We charge £3.50 commission.
   Customer: Hmm. I'll think about it, thanks.
c Clerk: One euro will get you 67 pence.
   Customer: Yes, that's OK. Here's my passport.
d Clerk: One US dollar is 109 Japanese yen.
   Customer: I think I'll leave it, thank you.

34

e Today's exchange rate from dollars to euros is .75.
f Yes, we can change traveller's cheques, but we charge £4.50 commission.
g No, we don't charge any commission.
h The exchange rate from pounds to dollars isn't very good today, I'm afraid.
i Yes, a hundred euros will get you seventy-five pounds today.

Unit 6

35

a (A and B = American)
   A: What's the matter?
   B: I don't feel very well. I've got a bad cough.
   A: Oh, dear. I'm sorry to hear that.
b (A and B = Australian)
   A: What's wrong?
   B: My back aches.
   A: Ah, poor you!
c A: Are you feeling OK?
   B: Not really. I think I've got a cold.
   A: I hope you feel better soon.

36

a (b, d and f = American)
   I walked home last night in the rain, and now I have a really bad cold.
b I've got a terrible cough. I think it's getting worse.
c Sorry, I can't play tennis tomorrow. I've got terrible backache.
d I spent too much time outside yesterday, and now I've got sunburn!
e I don't feel very well. I think I have a temperature.
f I don't know why, but I've got a bad sore throat this morning.

37 (Chemist = Indian)

a Chemist: Hello. Can I help you?
   Chemist: Yes, you can try this cream. It's very good.
   Chemist: Just a small amount, twice a day.
b Chemist: Hello. Can I help you?
   Chemist: Yes, you can try these throat tablets. They're very good.
   Chemist: Take one every four hours.
c Chemist: Can I help you?
   Chemist: Take these tablets. They'll soon bring your temperature down.
   Chemist: You can take two tablets twice a day.
d Chemist: Hello. Can I help you?
   Chemist: This medicine is very good.
   Chemist: Take one spoonful three times a day.
e Chemist: Can I help you?
   Chemist: You could try this cream. It's very good for sunburn.
   Chemist: You can use quite a lot. It's not very strong.

38 (Adli = Saudi Arabian; Fernando = Spanish)

Receptionist: Hello.
Adli: Oh, hello. I make an appointment please?*
Receptionist: Yes, of course. When would you like?
Adli: Thursday is OK. In the morning if possible.
Receptionist: OK … You can see Doctor Brown at 10.30. Is that all right?
Adli: Yes, that's OK.
Receptionist: And your name is…?
Adli: Adli Zaid. That's Z-A-I-D.
Receptionist: Thank you. That's fine.
Adli: So that's Doctor Brown on Thursday at 10.30.
Receptionist: That's right.
Adli: OK. Thank you. Bye.

Receptionist: Hello.
Fernando: I'd like to make an appointment please.
Receptionist: Certainly. Who's your doctor?
Fernando: Doctor Williams.
Receptionist: OK … Er, Doctor Williams is busy all day today but Wednesday at 3pm is possible.
Fernando: Great.
Receptionist: And you are …?
Fernando: Fernando Silva.
Receptionist: That's S-I-L-V-A?
Fernando: Yes, that's right.
Receptionist: OK. Thank you. I've put you in.

Fernando: So that's Wednesday at 3pm, with Doctor Williams.
Receptionist: Yes, that's fine.
Fernando: Thanks a lot. Bye.

*Did you notice?

Notice that Adli says *I make an appointment, please?* A native speaker would say *Can I make an appointment, please?* or *I'd like to make an appointment, please.*

39

1 doctor, water, pharmacy, tablet, sympathy
2 problem, important, conversation, patient, temperature
3 Have you got something for a headache? What have you got for a sore throat?
4 Take regular exercise.
   I was ill a week ago.
   Can I make an appointment, please?

40

a Hello. Doctor Park's surgery.
b When would you like to come?
c Doctor Park can see you at 4:30 on Thursday. Would that be OK?
d And what's your name please?
e OK, that's fine.

Receptionist: Yes, that's right. We'll see you on Thursday. Goodbye.

41

a Hmm. OK, well I think you have a very bad sore throat. I'll give you a prescription for some tablets. I want you to take two of these every day … that's one in the morning and one at night. Oh, and drink lots of water as well. That will help.
b (The doctor = Indian)
   Yes, well a problem like backache is always very hard to deal with … there are so many reasons why people get backache. However, it's painful, so I'll give you some cream. Use it at night before you sleep, and see me again next week.
c (The doctor = South African)
   Well, the good news is that I don't think it's the flu, but you do have a bad cold and cough. You don't need any medicine, just stay in bed and take it easy. Oh, and I wouldn't recommend going to work for three days or so.

Unit7

42 (Da-Ho = Chinese)

Check-in clerk: Can I have your ticket and passport, please?

Da-Ho: Yes, of course. Here you are.

Check-in clerk: Did you pack your bags yourself?

Da-Ho: Yes.

Check-in clerk: How many bags are you checking in?

Da-Ho: Just one. I'm taking this hand luggage.

Check-in clerk: Are there any sharp items in your hand luggage?

Da-Ho: No, there aren't.

Check-in clerk: Would you like an aisle seat or a window seat?

Da-Ho: A window seat if possible, please.

Check-in clerk: OK. Here you go. This is your boarding card. The flight leaves at 1.20. Go to Gate 17 around 12.30. Have a nice flight.

Da-Ho: Thank you.

43

a   Hello. Can I have your passport, please?

b   Thank you. Oh, and have you got your ticket?

c   Thank you. Did you pack your bags yourself?

d   How many bags are you checking in?

e   Are you taking any hand luggage on board?

f   Are there any sharp items in your hand luggage?

g   Would you like an aisle seat or a window seat?

Check-in: OK. Here you go. This is your boarding card. Your flight leaves at four o'clock. Enjoy your flight.

44 (Da-Ho = Chinese; Immigration officer = American)

Immigration officer: Where are you travelling from today?

Da-Ho: From London.

Immigration officer: What's the purpose of your visit?

Da-Ho: Business, I'm afraid. I have a meeting tomorrow.

Immigration officer: Do you have anything to declare?

Da-Ho: No, nothing to declare.

Immigration officer: Where are you going to stay?

Da-Ho: At the Orlando Hotel.

Immigration officer: How long are you going to stay in the country?

Da-Ho: Just three days. I go* Beijing on Monday.

Immigration officer: OK, that's all. Thank you very much. Enjoy your stay in LA.

Da-Ho: Thanks a lot.

☞*Did you notice?

Notice that the Da-Ho says *I go Bejing on Monday*. A native speaker would say *I go/ I'm going to Bejing on Monday*.

45 (Immigration officer = American)

a   Where are you travelling from today?

b   What's the purpose of your visit?

c   Do you have anything to declare?

d   Where are you going to stay?

e   How long are you going to stay in the country?

OK, that's all. Thank you very much. Enjoy your stay in LA.

46 (Mrs Hatano = Japanese; Eduardo = Brazilian; John = American)

a   Simon: Excuse me. Are you Mrs Hatano?

Mrs Hatano: Yes, I am.

Simon: Pleased to meet you. I'm from World Tours. I'm here to take you to your hotel.

Mrs Hatano: OK. Good.

Simon: How was your flight?

Mrs Hatano: It was fine, thank you.

Simon: May I take your bags?

Mrs Hatano: Yes. Thank you very much.

b   Eduardo: Hi, John. Great to see you.

John: Hi Eduardo.

Eduardo: Here. I'll take your bag.

John: Thanks. I'm exhausted!

Eduardo: Was the flight OK?

John: Yeah, not bad, thanks.

Unit8

47

a   Do you have a room with a view?

b   All our rooms are en-suite.

c   We'd like a double room, please.

d   I'm afraid we're fully booked.

e   Yes, we have a room available for those dates.

f   Does the price include breakfast?

g   Can I have your name please?

h   Yes, I've booked that for you now.

48 (Juan Carlos = Spanish)

Juan Carlos: Excuse me.

Receptionist: Yes, how can I help you?

Juan Carlos: How much is a single room, please?

Receptionist: A standard single is sixty euros a night.

Juan Carlos: I see. And do you have any non-smoking rooms?

Receptionist: Yes, we do. All our rooms are non-smoking.

Juan Carlos: Oh. Are the rooms air-conditioned?

Receptionist: Yes, they are.

Juan Carlos: That's good. And is breakfast included?

Receptionist: No, breakfast is ten euros extra, but it's very good.

Juan Carlos: OK. Oh, and one last question. How far is it to the city centre from here?

Receptionist: Around two kilometres. It's a nice walk.

Juan Carlos: OK. Thank you very much for your help.

Receptionist: You're welcome.

49

Receptionist: Here's your room key. Your room is 254.

Guest: Thank you. It's a non-smoking room, isn't it?

Receptionist: Yes, that's correct. All our rooms are non-smoking.

Guest: Good. And breakfast starts at six thirty, doesn't it?

Receptionist: Yes, six thirty, that's right. Enjoy your stay.

50 (Aiko = Japanese; Ulrike = German; Rashid = from UAE; Marc = French)

Aiko: It's a really nice room, but it's a bit small. There's a mini-bar, though, which is great, and the TV has lots of movie channels.

Ulrike: Yes, the room's fine, thanks. It's pretty big and there's a nice balcony. There's also a hair dryer and an iron and ironing board, which is useful because a lot of my clothes need ironing.

Rashid: Yeah, it's good. I like it. It has a bath and shower, which is great because I always like to have a bath in the evening … and there's a nice view over the park. I can make tea and coffee, too.

Marc: The bed's huge. It's the biggest I've ever seen! Oh, and the air-conditioning is really good, too. That's so important in hot weather.

51 (Receptionist = Brazilian)
You can have breakfast from 7 to 10 every morning in the café over there, next to the gift shop. There is an Italian restaurant on the third floor, and the bar is open until 2am. We have a fitness centre on the top floor, and there's a swimming pool up there too.

52 (Receptionist = Brazilian)
1 Normally it's at 11, but you can have a late check-out until 2pm if you like.
2 Yes, we'll deliver it to your room. What paper would you like?
3 No problem. Just tell us the time you want us to call you.
4 Yes, it's a next day service. Put it in the bag and the maid'll collect it.
5 Yes, we have 24-hour room service.
6 We don't, I'm afraid, but there is an internet café around the corner.

53
Do you have internet access?
What time do you serve breakfast?
Do you have any non-smoking rooms?
What restaurants do you have?
Do you have a room with a view?

Unit9

54 (Clerk = Chinese)
Clerk: Next, please.
Stephan: Can I have a single to the city centre, please?
Clerk: A single? Of course, here you are.
Stephen: Oh, how long does it take?
Clerk About thirty minutes.
Stephen: What time's the next train?
Clerk: The next train's at 3.15.
Stephen: Er, which platform does it leave from?
Clerk: Platform 3. Over there.
Stephen: Thank you.
Clerk: You're welcome.

55
a Next, please.
b A return? Of course, here you are.
c That's £18.20, please.
d About forty-five minutes.
e The next train's at 1.15.

Clerk: Platform 9. Have a good journey.

56 (i = from New Zealand; j = South African)
1
a The 7.45 train to Edinburgh will leave from Platform 1. Platform 1 for the 7.45 to Edinburgh.

b The 7.49 service to York will depart from Platform 3.
c The train to Cambridge will depart from Platform 9 at 8.15. That's Platform 9 for the 8.15 service to Cambridge.
d The 7.50 intercity service to Liverpool Lime Street is delayed. This train will now leave at 8.10, from Platform 7.
e The 7.45 train to Belfast will leave from Platform 1. Platform 1 for the 7.45 to Belfast.
f The 5.49 service to Bristol will depart from Platform 3.
g The train to Newcastle will depart from Platform 9 at 8.15. That's Platform 9 for the 8.15 service to Newcastle.
h The 10.50 intercity service to Liverpool Lime Street is cancelled. We apologize for any inconvenience this may cause.
i The 9.10 coach service to Wellington will leave from Bay 12. That's Bay 12 for the 9.10 service to Wellington.
j Passengers waiting for the 3.05 service to Cape Town please go to Bay 3. That's Bay 3 for the 3.05 service to Cape Town.

57 (Stacey = South African)
I've got a really busy day today. At 8.30 I have a breakfast meeting with Mrs Jenson at ALC. Then I have to be back by ten for a meeting with Bob and Sean. Before lunch around quarter to twelve I'm seeing Helen to go through the sales report. Then it's off to lunch at one with Dan Chester. He's from Karanco. After lunch I've got to go to GEO International for another meeting. That's from 2.30 to around four. And finally it's back to collect Janet from school at 5.15. What a day!

58
a (A = American)
A: You go along Nether Street and turn right.
B: OK.
A: And the internet café is on your left.
B: Thank you.

b (B = American)
A: Can you tell me where the subway is, please?
B: Sure. You turn left and go past the bank. The subway's on the left.
A: Thanks very much.

c (A = American; B = Indian)
A: So you go along Station Road and turn right onto Market Street.
B: So, turn right onto Market Street.
A: Yeah. And then go straight along Market Street and you'll see it on your left. It's on the corner of Northern Road.
B: Thank you.

d (A = American; B = Brazilian)
A: Well, the quickest way is to go out onto Station Road and then turn right straight away onto Broadway.
B: Broadway?
A: Yes, that's right. Go along Broadway, and then turn right into North Passage. You'll see it on the left.
B: Thanks very much.

e (A = American)
A: Oh, it's on the High Street, so from Station Road you want to turn right onto Nether Street, then take the second road on the left. That's High Street.
B: OK? And is it far?
A: Not really. Once you're on High Street you just follow the road until you get to the corner with Old Roman Way. Then you'll see it on the left.

f (A = American)
A: OK, the quickest way is to turn right onto Broadway, then turn left into Willow Way.
B: OK.
A: Then go along Willow Way until you reach Oak Street?
B: Oak Street?
A: Yes, then turn left into Oak Street. Go along Oak Street, then straight over Ribbon Hill into Archway.
B: So, straight over Ribbon Hill into Archway?
A: Yes, go along Archway until you reach Museum Street, then you'll see it in front of you.
B: Thank you very much.

59
A: Go along here and turn left. The bus station is on the corner.
B: On the corner?
A: Yes.

A: The post office is past the bank on the left.
B: OK, so past the bank on the left?
A: Yes.

60
a Go along here, and turn left. The train station's on the right.
b The post office is just there, on the corner.
c I think the police station is on Park Lane.
d Go past the supermarket and the library's on the left.
e The train leaves at 4.30.
f There's a bus at 9.45.

61 (speakers a, d and e = American)

a Can you tell me where the subway is, please?
b Where's the bus station, please?
c Excuse me. How do I get to Henry's Wine Bar?
d Can you tell me where the supermarket is, please?
e Excuse me. How do I get to the Tourist Information Office?

Unit 10

62

a Are there any good markets here?
b What museums do you recommend?
c Where's the best place to go shopping?
d Are there any temples I can visit near here?
e Is there a guided tour I can go on?

63 (Assistant = Chinese)

1 Yes, Wong Tai Sin temple is very popular. It's about five minutes from here.
2 Yes, there are lots. Hong Kong is famous for markets. Stanley market is very popular and there's a good night market in Temple Street, too.
3 Yes. A tour bus leaves from just across the road, every fifteen minutes.
4 You can find good shop everywhere*, but Central district and Causeway Bay are worth trying first.
5 There are many good ones. There's the Space Museum, the Science Museum, there's a very good art museum and the Horse Racing Museum is popular too.

☞*Did you notice?

Notice that the Tourist Information Office assistant says *You can find good shop everywhere*. A native speaker would say *You can find good shops everywhere*.

64

Jim: So, this is our first day in New York. What shall we do?
Denise: Well, how about going to the Metropolitan Museum of Art? People say it's really good.
Jim: I'd rather not do that today. The weather's great. I want to be outside.
Denise: OK, well … why don't we go to the Statue of Liberty?
Jim: That's a good idea. And afterwards what about going to Central Park?
Denise: Sure. That sounds great. Oh, and I want to go to Times Square as well.
Jim: That's fine with me. Let's go there first. It's not far from here.

65 (Giulia = Italian)

Bill: OK. So this is called The Rocks. The guidebook says this is where white people first arrived in 1788.
Giulia: Right. Let's look around …
Bill: … Well, here's Sydney Opera House. It says here it opened in 1973. What do you think?
Giulia: How amazing! It looks still very modern.*
Bill: Let's go in and have a look …
Giulia: … Here we are. The Botanic Gardens.
Bill: How beautiful! There's a guided walk starting soon. Shall we go on that? …
Giulia: OK.
Giulia: Darling Harbour. The guidebook says there's a great view from here.
Bill: Yes, look! It's fantastic! Wait a minute, I want to take some photos of this …
Giulia: … Here it is. The Aquarium. Ah, it's huge!
Bill: Yes. It's one of the biggest in the world, apparently. Where's the entrance?
Giulia: Over there. But let's sit here for a minute. I'm exhausted! …

☞*Did you notice?

Notice that Giulia says *It looks still very modern*. A native speaker would say *It still looks very modern*.

66

That's a good idea.
That sounds great.
I don't really want to do that.
I'd rather do something else.
I don't mind.
It's up to you.
That's fine with me.
That sounds fun.

67 (The speaker = Spanish)

We are now in Placa Catalunya, at the centre of the city … And to your left you can see the start of Las Ramblas, a long street of two kilometres, where you can find shops, bars, restaurants, markets, great theatres … everything! You should walk down Las Ramblas while you are in Barcelona.
… Ladies and gentlemen, we are coming to one of the most famous sights of Barcelona, La Casa Batlló. It is an excellent example of modernist art. Antoni Gaudí designed the building, and everything inside, even the furniture …
… Here on the right you can see Casa Milà, also called La Pedrera, which is perhaps the most famous of all his buildings. There is no straight line anywhere, and even the walls aren't straight, but like a wave. It was built between 1905 and 1910 as an apartment block and office building …
… And now we can see Sagrada Familia, the unfinished cathedral of Barcelona. Building began in 1882 and they are still working to finish it. Gaudí spent over 40 years working on this cathedral. On the right you can see …

Review 1

68

1 Do you need any help?
2 Are you ready to order?
3 Pleased to meet you.
4 Hello. How's it going?
5 How many stamps would you like?
6 Can I have your boarding card, please?
7 This is my husband, Miguel.
8 What do you think of the castle?
9 I'm going on holiday tomorrow.
10 Bye for now.

69

1 a Excuse me. Where's the cash desk?
   b Sorry, how much are these?
   c OK. I'll take it.
2 a I'll speak to you later.
   b Please call me soon.
   c Is it OK if I use your phone?
3 a You should take these tablets.
   b Have you got something for a cough?
   c Can I have a prescription, please?
4 a Pleased to meet you, too.
   b Great music, isn't it?
   c How about you?
5 a I think I'll leave it.
   b I'll take these.
   c How much are these?
6 a I'll have the soup and then a steak.
   b Can I have the bill, please?
   c Can I order now?
7 a Can you give me a cheque, please?
   b Do you accept cheques?
   c Can I pay this cheque in, please?
8 a Helen, I'd like you to meet some of my friends.
   b Pleased to meet you, Helen.
   c You don't know my friends, Helen.
9 a Where were these jeans made?
   b What size are these jeans?
   c How much are these jeans?
10 a Yes, that's fine.
    b I'll think about it, thanks.
    c Can I change this into euros, please?

CD2 Work and Study

Unit 11

2 (Rita and customer a = South African)

a Rita: Hello. Do you need any help?
Customer: Yes, thanks. I'm here to see Mr Egbe. Erm, where's his office, please?
Rita: It's along here. Let me show you the way.
Customer: Oh, thank you very much.

b Rita: May I help you?
Customer: Er, yes. Do you have a price list?
Rita: Yes, we do. Here you are.
Customer: Thanks a lot.
Rita: I'll give you a new catalogue, too.

c Customer: Hello.
Rita: Yes, can I help you?
Customer: Thanks. I'm looking for a television. What special offers have you got?
Rita: We have a good one over here. Shall I show you?
Customer: Yes, please.
Rita: It's in the sale at the moment.

3

a Excuse me. How much are these?
b Sorry, but I don't know where I put my catalogue.
c Can you tell me where the sales office is, please?
d This pen is broken, I'm afraid.
e This box is heavy!

4 (Rita and Chris = South African)

a Chris: Hello. Do you know where Charles is?
Rita: I think he's at lunch.
Chris: Oh, well. Can you ask him to call me when he gets in?
Rita: OK. I'll tell him.

b Judith: Is Cynthia there?
Rita: No, she isn't, I'm afraid.
Judith: Hmm. We've got a meeting this afternoon, but Meeting Room 1's busy so can you tell her we've changed it to Meeting Room 4?
Rita: OK. I'll tell her.

c Chris: Where's Kevin?
Rita: I don't know, I'm afraid.
Chris: Well, I need this month's sales report. Erm, can you tell him to email it as soon as possible? It's very important.
Rita: The sales report? Sure, no problem.

d Judith: I'm trying to find Sue. Have you seen her?
Rita: Not since this morning. I think she's with a client.
Judith: Well, we have a meeting at two o'clock. Remind her if you see her, will you?
Rita: Yes, OK, Judith. Two o'clock. I'll remind her when I see her.

e Chris: I can't find the key for the store cupboard. Do you know where it is?
Rita: I think Joseph had it.
Chris: Ah, well, can you tell him I need it?
Rita: OK.

5 (Sue and Charles = American; Rita = South African)

1 Sue: Hi, Rita.
Rita: Oh, hi, Sue. Judith came in. She said don't forget the meeting at two o'clock.
Sue: No, I won't forget.

2 Cynthia: Hi Rita, any messages for me?
Rita: Yes. Judith said the meeting this afternoon is in Meeting Room 4, not 1, OK?
Rita: OK. Thanks.

3 Joseph: Hi, Rita.
Rita: Oh, hi, Joseph. Chris says have you got the key for the store cupboard?
Joseph: Oh, yes. It's in my pocket!

4 Charles: Right, I think that's everything.
Rita: Oh, there's one more thing. Chris wants you to call him.
Charles: Oh, OK. Thanks.

5 Rita: Has Chris managed to contact you?
Kevin: No, why?
Rita: Oh, he wants you to email this month's sales report as soon as possible. He said it's very important.
Kevin: Oh no, I forgot! Thanks for telling me.

6 (John = American)

a Hello. It's Mr Brown. Can you tell David to call me when you see him?
b Hi, John here. Can you ask Chris to bring this week's business report to my office?
c Hi. It's Anna. If you see Helen, please tell her to take the store key back to reception.
d Hi, Martin here. We've got a meeting in Room 2 at three o'clock. Can you tell Lisa, please? I can't find her.
e Hello. Mr Brown here again. Can you tell George that the report is for January the third, not the eighth? Thanks.

7

a Oh, and can you send an email to Helen? Tell her there's a meeting next Tuesday … I'm not sure she knows.
b Can you call David Green and ask him to send the report? I don't know why I haven't got it yet.
c Great, so that's it. Oh, one more thing. Could you ask Bob if he can come at five? It's late but that's the only time I can see him.
d Would you mind emailing John at head office for me? Ask him to come to next week's presentation.
e Please can you make six copies of the Clarkson file? I need it by lunchtime.

8

a A: Well, I'd better go now.
B: Well, it was great to see you. Thanks very much for coming.
b A: I have to leave now, I'm afraid.
B: Well, I hope to see you again soon. Have a safe journey.
c I have to go now to catch my train.
d Well, it's time for me to go.
e I must go now. My taxi's waiting.
f Well, I'd better go. It's been a very useful meeting.

Unit 12

9

a
Assistant: Hello?
Customer: Hello. Do you sell office furniture?
Assistant: Yes, we do.
Customer: I'm looking for a desk.
Assistant: Oh, we have a wide range of desks.
Customer: Great. Can you send me a catalogue so I can have a look?

b
Assistant: Hello, Hadley Office Supplies?
Customer: Hi. Er, do you sell photocopiers?
Assistant: No, I'm afraid we don't.
Customer: Oh, OK. Thanks.

c
Assistant: Hello?
Customer: Hi. Do you have any printer cartridges?
Assistant: Yes, we do. We sell all the main brands.
Customer: OK, thanks. I'll come in.
Assistant: All right. Bye.
Customer: Bye.

d

Assistant: Hello, can I help you?

Customer: Hi. I'm looking for some large A3 size envelopes. Do you have any?

Assistant: Yes, we do.

e

Assistant: Hello?

Customer: Hello. Do you sell computers?

Assistant: No, I'm afraid we don't. Sorry.

Customer: That's OK. Bye.

🔊 **10** (d = American)

a   Oh, hello. Yes, er… Do you repair computers?

b   The price is a bit high. Can you give me a discount?

c   Oh, and one more thing. Do you charge for delivery?

d   It's very urgent so could you send it by special delivery, please?

e   I need it quite soon. When can you deliver?

🔊 **11** (Speaker = Indian)

1   It's free if you live locally, otherwise we charge £20.

2   The next delivery will go out on Friday. Is that OK?

3   Yes, of course. It'll be £15 extra, though.

4   Yes, we do. Bring it in and we'll take a look at it.

5   I'm sorry. That's the best price we can offer you.

🔊 **12**

Customer: Hello. Do you sell A3 paper?

Assistant: Yes we do. We sell all sizes of paper.

Customer: I'd like to order three boxes of A3, please.

Assistant: Certainly. Three boxes. Anything else?

Customer: No, that's everything. Can you deliver?

Assistant: Yes, we deliver free of charge.

🔊 **13** (f–j = American)

a   Can you deliver this next Wednesday?

b   Could you please reduce the price?

c   Could you send this by airmail?

d   Can you repair this computer?

e   Can you keep this for me until Tuesday?

f   Could you deliver this next Saturday?

g   Can you give me a discount?

h   Could you send this by airmail?

i   Can you repair this photocopier today?

j   Can you keep this for me until Wednesday?

🔊 **14** (Nihar = Indian)

Assistant: Hello, Hadley Office Supplies.

Nihar: Hello. I'd like to order some office furniture, please?

Assistant: OK. Do you have an account with us?

Nihar: Yes. ABS Printers.

Assistant: Let me see … ABS Printers. Yes, that's fine. Erm, what items did you want to order?

Nihar: Two large desks. I think the catalogue number is 3743.

Assistant: 3743 … large desk … That's right. They're £175 each. Two of those, you say?

Nihar: Yes. Thanks.

Assistant: Anything else?

Nihar: Yes, a chair. It's number 984a.

Assistant: Just a moment … 984a … Ah yes. One executive chair, £78?

Nihar: That's right.

Assistant: OK. That's ordered for you. Is that everything?

Nihar: Yes, that's it.

Assistant: OK. So that will be £502.90, including VAT.

Nihar: Could you deliver on Friday?

Assistant: Yes, no problem.

Nihar: Great. Thanks a lot.

🔊 **15** (Emily and Tom = from New Zealand)

Emily: So, which one do you think is better, Tom?

Tom: Well, the T150's cheaper …

Emily: Yes, but it's very big.

Tom: And the X80's quicker, isn't it?

Emily: Hmm. That's true. But it's the wrong colour. I don't like black.

Tom: So, which do you want to buy? Come on. Make your mind up!

Emily: OK. I think I'll get the T150.

🔊 **16**

a   Do you want the blue one or the black one?

b   Do you want to pay by cash or credit card?

c   Would you like the T150 or the X80?

d   Do you want to order one or two?

e   Is the delivery date the 5th or the 6th?

Unit 13

🔊 **17** (Operator and Jennifer = American)

Operator: Thank you for calling Denco Computing. Paul speaking. How may I help you?

Jennifer: Hello. Hi, it's Jennifer Ratby here. Can I speak to David Henshaw, please?

Operator: Hold the line. I'll put you through.

David: Good afternoon. This is David Henshaw.

Jennifer: David? Hi, it's Jennifer Ratby here.

David: Oh, hello Jennifer. What can I do for you?

Jennifer: It's about the contract. When do you think it will be ready?

David: I'll send it tomorrow. Is that OK with you?

Jennifer: Sure. Thanks a lot. Say, is Charles there? I need to talk to him about next year's prices.

David: I'm afraid he's out of the office at the moment.

Jennifer: How about Kevin? Is he in? I need to arrange a meeting.

David: Yes, but he's on another call right now. Would you like to leave a message?

Jennifer: Could you ask him to call me back when he's free?

David: No problem. Thanks for calling.

🔊 **18** (a = Chinese; b = American; d = South African)

a   Can you say that I called. My name's Shuang Liang.

b   And tell him I'll call on the seventeenth …

c   So it's next Friday and not the one after that that I need the report by, you see.

d   This is Mr Pieterse speaking.

e   Please say the systems analysis is nearly finished.

🔊 **19**

1   /ei/ /iː/ /e/ /ai/ /əu/ /uː/ /aː/

2   a b c d e f g h i j k l m n o p q r s t u v w x y z

🔊 **20**

a   My name's Henman. That's H-E-N-M-A-N.

b   My first name's Sophia. It's spelt S-O-P-H-I-A.

c   I'm Jonathon. That's spelt J-O-N-A-T-H-O-N.

d   This is Thomson here. That's T-H-O-M-S-O-N.

e   I'm Mary Anne. M-A-R-Y A-N-N-E.

f   B-R-A-D-S-H-A-W

g   N-A-V-Y-K-A-R-N

h   S-U-K-R-I-S-H-N-A

i   M-O-H-A-M-M-E-D

j   I-G-N-A-C-I-O

21 (Susan = American)

a Hello, it's David Brown here. Um. I'm calling about the contract. I have a few questions and I think we should meet. I'm free on Friday so if you have time for lunch, let's say 12.45? Please call me to confirm. My number is 0207-9845-6109. Thanks. Bye.

b Hello Geena? Are you there? It's Susan here from Accounts. Listen, I can't find your sales report for the Shelford project. Do you know where it is? I need it before the sales meeting at four this afternoon. Please call me as soon as you get this message. I'm on extension 790. Thanks!

c Robert Macintyre here, that's M-A-C-I-N-T-Y-R-E, from Shell International. Richard Thomas suggested I speak to you about the new project you are working on for us. We need to talk about prices. Can you call me on 0190-456-0280 when you get this message? I'll be in the office until 3.15 this afternoon. Or you can reach me on my mobile after 6.30 this evening. The number is 07967-7635423. Thank you.

22 (b, d, g = American)

a 020-7834-5633
b 212-490-3021
c 020-8934-0251
d 212-691-4078
e 0161-310-4639
f 01482-886-291
g 810-5390-2681
h 020-7344-1920
i 02-2964-4930
j 512-034-763
k 011-336-5621
l 07978-462-0988

23 (b = Indian; d = Italian)

a This is the voicemail for Peter Bradshaw. Please leave a message.

b Hi, this is Sagar. Please leave a message and I'll get back to you.

c This is Hadley Office Supplies. I'm afraid there's no one free to take your call at the moment. Please leave a message.

d This is the voicemail for Maria Vestri. Please leave a message.

Unit 14

24 (Amy = Chinese)

a Hello everyone, and welcome. My name is George Anderson and the purpose of this talk is to explain our new website.

b Hello. It's great to see you all here today. I'm Amy Lee, and in this presentation I want to show you our marketing strategy for this year.

c Good morning, everyone. Today I'm going to talk to you about the new ordering system we have here.

25

To start with I'll talk about the new computer program we are using. Then I'll explain how to search for a product. After that I'll show you how to order, and finally I'll tell you how to contact us if you have a problem.

26

OK, so now I'm going to show you how to order. Well, thanks to our new ordering system, it's very easy. First, type in the customer's name and address here … Second, choose the product the customer wants to order from this list … Third, select the quantity the customer wants … and lastly enter your sales number. There, that's it!

27

OK, so that's how the new ordering system will work. We started developing it three years ago, and I hope you'll agree there are many benefits to using a new computer system like this one. When the system is ready, it will save everybody a lot of time. The new system will also be more efficient, and there won't be so many mistakes. It should save us money, too. So, in conclusion, this new ordering system will make all of our lives a lot easier. Thanks for coming. I hope you have found the talk useful.

28 (Amy = Chinese)
To sum up, sales this year are good, and they should continue to grow. Thank you very much for listening.

29

a Hmm. I'm not sure I agree.
b That's a very good point.
c I don't think that's exactly right.
d I couldn't agree more.
e I think you may be wrong about that.
f I think you're right.

30

Anna: What did you think of the presentation?
James: I liked it. I think it was very interesting.
Anna: Really? I don't agree. I think it was a bit boring.

James: Oh dear. Why do you think that?
Anna: Because there was nothing new in it.

31

a Did you enjoy the talk?
b I thought that was very interesting. What do you think?
c I really enjoyed that presentation. How about you?
d What did you think of the talk?
e That was interesting, wasn't it?
f I didn't think that presentation was very good. How about you?

Unit 15

32 (Ana = Brazilian)

Ana: … Erm, but because of the United Nations EFA programme, the situation for kids has got a lot better recently.
Philip: Uh, sorry, can you say a bit more about that please, Ana?
Ana: Sure. The UN have a special programme called EFA, which stands for Education for All, and one of its goals is to make sure children everywhere have free primary education.
Philip: I see. So that programme is for all countries around the world?
Ana: Yes, but this latest report is for Africa and Asia. It says there are 20 million more children in primary schools than there were around ten years ago.

33

a The biggest cause is lack of funding by some governments.
b I think poor management is the biggest problem facing primary education.
c And so these unrealistic promises create false hope.
d Many college students decide to drop out before they finish their studies.
e It's interesting that girls do better at secondary education than boys.

34 (Kate = American; Teresa = Italian)

Sam: … So, to sum up then, computers will definitely become more important in both what we learn and how we study. Now, are there any questions?
Kate: Yes, Sam. I have a question.
Sam: Go ahead, Kate.
Kate: I'd like to ask you about computers in schools. Do you think that computers will one day replace teachers in the classroom?
Sam: Well, in my opinion, no. There are some things you can't learn from computers.

Kate: I don't agree. If you ask me, everyone will learn at home, on a computer. There won't be any schools anymore! What do you think, Teresa?

Teresa: The idea it's interesting*, Kate, but I'm not sure I agree. I can't imagine a world with no schools. Children need to learn from each other, as well as from a computer!

Sam: That's a good point, Teresa. I agree. There will always be schools because …

☞*Did you notice?

Notice that Teresa says *The idea it's interesting*. A native speaker would probably say *It's an interesting idea*.

35

a   There are too many exams.
b   Teaching is a very hard job.
c   Exams are a good way of testing students.
d   Governments shouldn't tell teachers what to teach.
e   All parents should pay for their children's education.
f   Children should start school at the age of four.

36

a   Do you think that the government should spend more on education?
b   Do you agree that education should be free to everyone?
c   Do you think children have the right to a good education?
d   Do you think that children should learn about politics at school?
e   Do you agree that schools should teach religion?
f   Do you think poor families should get money to send their children to school?

37

A: … So I think that tourism, although it has its benefits, basically it …
B: Sorry, do you mind if I interrupt?
A: Can you wait a minute while I finish? So while tourism has its benefits, in many parts of the world it creates a lot of problems for local communities and the local environment.
C: Can I say something here?
A: Sure, go ahead.
C: I think tourism brings a lot of benefits to a local community. For example, there are a lot of people who make money from tourism.
B: Sorry, but can I make a point?
A: Yes, of course.

B: A lot of the money from tourism doesn't go to the local people. It goes to large hotels and tour companies.

Unit 16

38   (Yuri = Russian; Monika = German)

Yuri: Have you got your schedule for this term, Monika?

Monika: Yes, Yuri, I have. It's going to be quite hard!

Yuri: Really? What subjects do you take?*

Monika: I've got Culture Studies, on Tuesdays and Thursdays at 8.30.

Yuri: Oh, 8.30! That's early. Do you have any classes after that?

Monika: Yes. Straight after that at 10 I have a class on Social Change.

Yuri: That sounds OK. Do you have the afternoon free?

Monika: Yes, but only Tuesdays and Thursdays. On Mondays, Wednesdays and Fridays I've got Language Development, at two o'clock.

Yuri: That sounds interesting. What other classes do you have?

Monika: I've got Education on Monday morning, at 9.40, and Communication Studies on Wednesdays and Fridays at 10.

Yuri: Wow. That's a lot of classes.

Monika: I know. I hope they'll be good!

☞*Did you notice?

Notice that Yuri says *What subjects do you take?* A native speaker would say *What subjects are you taking?*

39

a   Hello. Can I help you?
b   It starts next Monday, that's the fourth of September.
c   There are five classes a week.
d   Classes are on Monday to Friday, from nine till twelve.
e   They're in room 2A.

Secretary: It's Mr Price. OK? Bye.

40   (The speaker = American)

OK, now before you go I want to tell you about some special lectures this month. Dr Grimshaw will give a lecture on Study Skills in Room 173 on the 12th. That's Tuesday 12th in Room 173. I recommend that all new students attend this lecture. Also, on the 23rd, we have a guest speaker. Mr Collins from the British Council will be here to talk about Life and Culture in the UK. That's of interest to everyone so I recommend you all go to the Lecture Hall for that … and on

the 26th you can hear Professor Kaminski from Moscow State University talk on The Future of Computer Languages. That should be a very interesting talk for any Computer Science students, and that's in the Theatre. I'll put full details of these events and some others on the Student Noticeboard so …

41   (a = American; e = Australian)

a   OK, so for homework I want you to do the grammar and pronunciation exercises on page 28. Do this tonight, please, because we'll look at the answers tomorrow afternoon.
b   Over the weekend I want you to write a 2,000 word essay on Language and Culture, and give it to me first thing on Monday morning.
c   OK, so this week I want you to read five articles on Language Development. Here is the reading list. Please do this in time for the seminar on Wednesday 17th.
d   Right, listen everyone. The details of this term's assignment are on my website. We'll discuss this more next week, but basically I want you to work in groups of three to prepare a presentation on The Future of the English Language. As I say, all the information is on my website. The deadline for this is Monday 21st.
e   Homework is to prepare a one-minute talk. The title of the talk is How to be a successful language learner. We'll have the presentations next Friday, so make sure you're ready by then.

42   (Dr Gupta = Indian)

Mike: Dr Gupta.

Dr Gupta: Yes?

Mike: Er, I'm sorry, but I don't think I can hand the mid-term report in on time.

Dr Gupta: I see. Why not?

Mike: I've been ill this week and I couldn't do any work. But I'm better now.

Dr Gupta: OK, so when do you think you can do it?

Mike: Well, I'll start today. I have the reading list. I'll go to the library this afternoon after class.

Dr Gupta: It will take you a bit of time to do all the reading. Well, what about next Friday?

Mike: You mean Friday 27th?

Dr Gupta: Yes. Can you do it by then?

Mike: That should be OK. Thanks a lot.

43 (Dr Gupta = Indian)

Dr Gupta: It will take you a bit of time to do all the reading. Well, what about next Friday?

Mike: You mean Friday 27th?

44

a Please hand this in by Wednesday.
b I want you to complete the report by Friday 3rd.
c Do you think you can finish by the end of next week?
d I'll need this from you on Monday 17th.
e OK, can you do it before lunchtime tomorrow?

Review2

45 (3, 5 and 7 = American; 6 = Russian)

1 Hello. Can I speak to Miss Jenkins, please?
2 Could you repair this, please?
3 I think that presentation was really boring.
4 I don't like my Cultural Studies class this term.
5 In my opinion parents should be more responsible for their children's education.
6 Can you say I phoned? My name is Yuri Borzakovsky.
7 When can you deliver?
8 Let me show you the way.
9 Would you like to leave a message?
10 What did you think of the talk?

46 (5 = Spanish)

1 a How are you?
   b How about you?
   c How do you do?
2 a It's not a problem. I'll do it soon.
   b I'm sorry, but I'm afraid I haven't done my homework.
   c I'm sorry I'm late.
3 a What do you mean exactly?
   b Can you speak more slowly, please?
   c I'm not sure I agree.
4 a Sorry, I need some help.
   b Show me to the reception, please.
   c Excuse me. Can you tell me where the reception is, please?
5 a Who are you?
   b Hi, I'm Miguel. What's your name?
   c Can I help you?
6 a Certainly. I'll find one for you.
   b Let me show you the way.
   c Do you want any help?

7 a Can you ask Yolanda to call me?
   b Tell Yolanda to call me asap.
   c Sorry, but I want Yolanda to call me.
8 a You can't use the photocopier. I need to use it.
   b Stop using the photocopier. I need to use it.
   c Please don't use the photocopier. I need to use it.
9 a Repair this photocopier.
   b Would you repair a photocopier?
   c Do you repair photocopiers?
10 a Shall I help you?
    b I'll do it straight away.
    c Let me do that for you.

Answer key

Unit 1

Get ready to listen and speak

○ *Your own answers.*

A

1 Conversation a – picture 2, Conversation b – picture 1
2 I'm Samantha.   My name is Vladimir Petrov.
My name's Yoko Shirai.
3 Conversation b is more formal.
4 d Formal   e Formal   f Informal   g Informal

B

Daniela is from Italy. She's a nurse. She lives in Rome.
Joshua is from Canada. He's a sales manager. He lives in Vancouver.
Shizuka is from Japan. She's a science teacher. She lives in Tokyo.

Focus on saying hello

1 a Oh, not too **bad**, thanks.
  b Hi there. How are **things**?
     Fine, thanks.
  c Good morning. **How** are you?
     I'm very **well**, thank you.
2 Conversation c is formal.

Sound smart

2 c 1   d 1   e 2   f 2   g 2

C

1 b 1   c 3   d 2
2 *Your own answers. Possible answers:*
  b I'm looking forward to the weekend.
  c Excuse me. Is anyone sitting here?
  d Lovely weather today, isn't it?

D

1 They talk about the weather, sport and their home towns.
2 b do c married d children e job f weekend
3 *Your own answers. Possible answers:*
  b I'm a teacher. c No. d No. e Yes, I do. f No, not really.
4 ask the same question
5 *Your own answers. Possible answers:*
  b I'm a teacher. What about you?
  c No. How about you?
  d No. How about you?
  e Yes, I do. What about you?
  f No, not really. What about you?

E

1 Oh yes. Oh really? That's interesting.

2 *Your own answers. Possible answers:*
  b Oh, really? Where are you going?
  c That's good. What job is it?
  d That's interesting. What sports do you like?
  e Oh, really? Who's playing?
  f How amazing! Does he like it?

Focus on saying goodbye

1 a See b Good c Bye
2 Conversation b is formal.

Unit 2

Get ready to listen and speak

○ *Your own answers.*
○ *Your own answers.*
○ jeans h a jacket c a shirt f shoes i shorts a
  a suit d a sweater e trousers g

A

1 a shirt and a jacket
2 b £20 c Yes (it's half price) d leather e Italy
  f no g medium h £140
3 b looking c much d try e take
4 b C c C d S e C

Focus on singular and plural

b are c Is d are e Are f are g is h is

B

1 Carlos shows he understands the assistant by saying 'Oh, right'
and 'Oh, OK'.
2 b 1   c 4   d 2   e 3
3 a I'll take it.   b I'll leave it.
4 *Your own answers. Possible answers:*
  b Oh, right. OK, I'll take it.   c Oh, OK. I'll leave it, thanks.
  d Oh, right. I'll leave it, thanks.   e Oh, right. I'll take them, then.
  f Oh, OK. Good. I'll take them.

Sound smart

2 e How <u>much</u> is this <u>hat</u>?
  f Are <u>these</u> shoes in the <u>sale</u>?
  g <u>Where's</u> the <u>cash</u> desk?
  h Can I pay by <u>cheque</u>?
  i Do you have this <u>shirt</u> in <u>medium</u>?
  j Where are the <u>changing</u> rooms, <u>please</u>?

Answer key

C

b False (it costs £120)   c False (it's made of wool)
d True (from Paris)   e False (Kumiko says 'It's a little expensive')
f False (The stallholder says 'the normal price for that in the shops is three hundred quid')   g True   h False (The stallholder says 'cash only')

D

1 b 6 c 5 d 3 e 1 f 2
2 b $40 c €50 d £16 e €70 f $18
3 b $19.90 c €189 d $17.50 e £29.95 f €19

E

1 b Excuse me. Could you help me, please?
c Do you think you could help me?
2 5 Oh, OK. Can I try them on?
1 Excuse me. Can you help me, please?
4 Er, let me have a look. Here it is. They're £35.
2 Yes, of course. How can I help?
3 How much are these trousers? I can't find the price.
6 Yes, of course. The changing rooms are over there.
4 *Your own answers. Possible answers*:
b Excuse me. Can you help me, please? What size is this skirt?
c Excuse me. Do you think you could help me? Have you got these in medium?
d Excuse me. Could you help me, please? Where are the changing rooms?
e Excuse me. Could you help me, please? Is this jacket in the sale?

Unit3

Get ready to listen and speak

○ *Your own answers.*
○ *Your own answers.*

A

1 b Customer c Waiter d Waiter e Customer f Waiter
g Customer h Customer i Customer
2 b 5 c 1 d 3 e 2
4 *Your own answers. Possible answers*:
b Yes, I am. Thank you.
c I'll have a green salad, please.
d I'll have fish and chips, please.
e Yes, please. I'll have the chocolate cake.

B

2 *Your own answers. Possible answers*:
b Can you tell me what Spaghetti Carbonara is, please?
c What's in the Mexican Chicken?
d Excuse me. What's Summer Fruits Pudding?

Sound smart

2 a UP b DOWN
3 b down c up d down e up f up g down
h down

C

1 b Tomato soup   c Chicken curry with rice   d Fruit salad
2 b not very good, a bit too salty
c a bit too spicy, too hot, the rice is good
d delicious, fresh, a bit too sweet

Focus on words describing food

1 b soft c salty d tough
2 ☺ delicious, excellent, really tasty
☺ all right, OK ☹ awful, not very good

D

2 *Your own answers. Possible answers*:
b How's your steak?
c Is the chicken nice? d What's the salad like?
e Is your spaghetti nice?
3 *Your own answers. Possible answers*:
b It's delicious! It's very tender, and quite spicy. The chips are really tasty, too.
c It's not very good, I'm afraid. It's a bit too sweet for me.
d It's all right.   e It's excellent. It's really sweet and creamy.

E

1 a double cheeseburger with medium fries and a small coffee.
2 $4.98.

Unit4

Get ready to listen and speak

○ *Your own answers.*
○ *Your own answers.*
○ *Your own answers.*

A

2 a I'd like you to meet, This is …
b Nice to meet you. Pleased to meet you.
c Nice to meet you, too.
d Please call me …
3 b Nice to meet you, too.
c Fine, thank you.
d Pleased to meet you, too.

B

1 b 2 c 5 d 7 e 6 f 1 g 3
2 2 h 3 c 4 b 5 d 6 e 7 g 8 a
3 b True c False   (The lounge is opposite the kitchen.) d
False (The toilet is at the bottom of the stairs.) e True f False
(Abigail's room is opposite her parents' room.) g True h True

Sound smart

2 d It's a big room with a view of the park.
e Teresa picked up the bag and took it upstairs.
f We left our coats in the kitchen.
g I'd like a cup of tea, please.

Focus on modal verbs
1 b 1 c 4 d 2
2 b don't have to   c have to   d can't   e can / have to
   f don't have to

C

1 2 bathroom   3 Paula's room   4 washing clothes
   5 using the phone   6 house key
2 a T (Anytime is OK.)
   b T (Please go in at seven.)
   c T (I'll wash your towels and sheets once a week.)
   d F (You can do your washing on Sundays.)
   e F (You can use the phone for local calls but not international calls.)
   f T (Please come back before midnight.)

D

2 *Your own answers. Possible answers*:
   Is it OK if I turn up the heating?
   Do you think I could go out with some friends tonight?
   Would you mind if I have a bath?
   is it OK if I use the washing machine?
   Do you think I could make a cup of tea?
3 *Your own answers. Possible answers*:
   b Do you think I could have a shower?
   c Would you mind if I make a cup of coffee?
   d Is it OK if I turn up the heating?
   e Do you think I could use the phone?

E

1 a great, fantastic, very friendly, really helpful, good fun
   b quite good, OK
   c terrible, not very kind, a bit boring
2 *Your own answers. Possible answers*:
   b Meals with the family are great and really good fun.
   c The family is very friendly and really helpful.
   d The weather is fantastic!
   e The school is OK. The classes are quite good.

Unit 5

Get ready to listen and speak
○ *Your own answers.*
○ *Your own answers.*
○ b 5 c 7 d 8 e 2 f 6 g 1 h 3

A

1 In a post office: a, c, f, g   In a bank: b, d, e
2 b bank account
   c letter to Mexico
   d cheque book
   e balance
   f parcel by registered mail
   g letter by special delivery

B

1 Proof of identity: passport, driving licence, ID card
   Proof of address: telephone or electricity bill, rental contract
   Other documents: letter from school/employer
2 take out money, pay in cash/cheques, have a cash card
3 b cash a cheque
   c transfer some money to his savings account
4 b write her address on the back of the cheque   c show his bank card

Focus on money
1 b send   c order   d cash   e exchange   f check
2 b 3 c 4 d 2 e 1

C

1 I'd like to a   I need to c   I want to b
2 b I'd like to withdraw $400.
   c I have to send some money abroad.
   d I'd like to open an account.
3 *Your own answers. Possible answers*:
   b I'd like to take out €200.
   c I want to deposit $400.
   d I need to transfer £1000 to a bank account in Mexico.
   e I want to open an account, please.

D

1 a send three postcards to France by airmail
   b send a parcel to Poland by airmail
   c send a letter to Japan
   d send a letter to Australia by special delivery
2 a £1.50   b £11.70   c £3   d £6

E

1 Customer c says *Can I send this letter by airmail please?*
   Customer b says *How much is it to send this parcel by airmail?*
   Customer c says *How long will it take?*
2 *Your own answers. Possible answers*:
   b I'd like seven 72 pence stamps, please.
   c How much will it cost to send three postcards to Italy?
   d How much will it cost to send this parcel to South Africa by surface mail?
   e I'd like to send this letter to Portugal by airmail. How long will it take?
   f Can you weigh this for me, please? I need to send it to Canada. How much will it cost to send it by airmail?
3 *Your own answers. Possible answers*:
   b No, it's not urgent.
   c How long will it take by surface mail?
   d OK. How much will it cost by airmail?
   e How long will it take by airmail?
   f OK. I'll send it by airmail.

F

2 a That's fine. Yes, that's OK.
   b I'll think about it, thanks. I think I'll leave it, thank you.
3 *Your own answers. Possible answers*:
   f I think I'll leave it, thank you.
   g Yes, that's OK. Can I change £200 into dollars, please?
   h OK. I'll think about it, thanks.
   i That's fine. I'd like to change €200 into pounds.

Answer key

Unit6

Get ready to listen and speak

- *Your own answers.*
- *Your own answers.*
- b 5 c 7 d 8 e 2 f 6 g 1 h 3

A

1 a I don't feel very well. I've got a bad cough.
   Oh, dear. I'm sorry to hear that.
 b What's wrong?
   My back aches.
   Ah, poor you!
 c Are you feeling OK?
   Not really. I think I've got a cold.
   I hope you feel better soon.

2 asking about someone's health: What's the matter?, What's wrong?, Are you feeling OK?
 explaining a health problem: I've got a …, My … aches,
 showing sympathy: Oh dear. I'm sorry to hear that., Ah, poor you!, I hope you feel better soon.

B

2 *Your own answers. Possible answers to all questions*:
 Oh dear. I'm sorry to hear that.   Poor you! How awful.
 I hope you feel better soon.   Oh dear. How awful.
 Oh dear. Poor you!

Focus on giving advice

When you feel very ill you …
should see a doctor.   should take some medicine.
shouldn't continue to work.   should go home and rest.
To keep healthy you …
should drink lots of water.   shouldn't smoke.
should eat fresh fruit and vegetables.
should exercise regularly.   shouldn't eat a lot of fried food.

C

2 *Your own answers. Possible answers*:
 b What have you got for a headache?
 c Have you got something for sunburn?
 d What have you got for a cough?
 e Have you got something for a cold?

3 *Your own answers. Possible answers*:
 b Have you got something for a sore throat?
   OK. How many should I take?
 c Yes. What have you got for a temperature?
   How often should I take them?
 d Yes. Have you got something for a cough?
   OK, great. How much should I take?
 e Yes. What have you got for sunburn?
   OK. How much should I use?

D

1 Adli Zaid: Thursday, 10.30, Dr Brown
 Fernando Silva: Wednesday, 3pm, Dr Williams

2 I'd like to make an appointment, please.

Sound smart

2 prob<u>l</u>em important conversation patient tempe<u>ra</u>ture

4 Take reg<u>u</u>lar exercise.   I w<u>a</u>s ill <u>a</u> week <u>a</u>go.
 Can I make <u>an</u> appointm<u>e</u>nt, please?

E

1 The expression they both use is <u>So that's</u>…

2 *Your own answers. Possible answers*:
 b On Thursday afternoon if possible.
 c Yes, that's fine.
 d *Your own name*
 e OK. So that's 4:30 on Thursday, with Doctor Park.

Focus on imperatives

1 To make the positive imperative, you use the base form of the verb.
 To make the negative imperative, you use *Don't* + base form of the verb

2 a Take b Don't go c Stay d Don't drink
 e Use f Try g Don't work

F

a 1 F 2 F (you should take one tablet twice a day) 3 T
b 1 T 2 F (use it at night) 3 F (you should go again next week)
c 1 F (the doctor doesn't think it's the flu) 2 T 3 T

Unit7

Get ready to listen and speak

- a 4 b 2 c 6 d 5 e 1 f 3
- b 3 c 4 d 1 e 2

A

2 a passport b pack your bags c checking d hand luggage
 e window

3 b Gate 17 c around 12.30

B

1 Da-Ho says *Here you are* and the check-in assistant says *Here you go*.

2 *Your own answers. Possible answers*:
 b Yes, here you are.
 c Yes, I did.
 d I've got two bags.
 e Yes, I've got one piece of hand luggage.
 f No.
 g I'd like a window seat, please.

C

1 4 Where are you going to stay?
 2 What's the purpose of your visit?
 1 Where are you travelling from today?
 5 How long are you going to stay in the country?
 3 Do you have anything to declare?

2 a False (He's there on business.) b True c True
 d False (He's going to stay at the Orlando Hotel.)
 e False (He's going to stay for three days.)

D

1 a NO   b YES   c YES

2 *Your own answers. Possible answers*:
   b Business.
   c No, nothing to declare.
   d At the Hilton Hotel.
   e For two weeks.

E

1 Where can I hire a car?
   Where can I find a bureau de change?
   Where's the bus station, please?
   How can I get to the city centre?
   Can you recommend a good hotel?

2 *Your own answers. Possible answers*:
   b Where can I find a bureau de change? / Where can I change some money?
   c Where's the bus station, please?
   d Where can I hire a car?
   e Can you recommend a good hotel in the city centre?
   f Where can I get a taxi, please?

Focus on locations

b 4   c 1   d 6   e 5   f 2

F

1 a 2   b 1

2 a Pleased to meet you. / May I take your bag? / Thank you very much.
   b Hi. Great to see you. / I'll take your bag. / Thanks.

3 Conversation a is formal and conversation b is informal.

Unit 8

Get ready to listen and speak

○ *Your own answers.*

○ *Your own answers.*

A

1 b Receptionist   c Guest   d Receptionist
   e Receptionist   f Guest   g Receptionist   h Receptionist

2 b non-smoking rooms
   c air-conditioned   d breakfast   e city centre

3 a €60   b Yes (all rooms are non-smoking)   c Yes
   d No (it's €10 extra)   e about two kilometres

B

2 2 Thank you. It's a non-smoking room, isn't it?
   4 Good. And breakfast starts at six thirty, doesn't it?
   5 Yes, six thirty, that's right. Enjoy your stay.
   3 Yes, that's correct. All our rooms are non-smoking.
   1 Here's your room key. Your room is 254.

4 *Your own answers. Possible answers*:
   b Breakfast is included, isn't it?
   c It's on the first floor, isn't it?
   d Dinner starts at eight, doesn't it?
   e It's a single room, isn't it?
   f It's got a shower, hasn't it?

Focus on making statements into questions

b hasn't it?   c isn't it?   d isn't it?
e hasn't it?   f isn't it?   g hasn't it?

C

1 a 2   b 4   c 1   d 3

2 Aiko: b, e, i   Ulrike: j, c   Rashid: a, d, h   Marc: g, f

D

1 The receptionist mentions: café, gift shop, restaurant, bar, fitness centre and swimming pool.

2 a False (it's from seven to ten)   b True   c False (it's on the third floor)   d True   e False (it's on the top floor)

3 2 f   3 b   4 e   5 c   6 a

E

2 *Your own answers. Possible answers*:
   b Sorry to bother you, but I asked for a room with a view, but this room has no view.
   c I'm afraid that the air-conditioning in here doesn't work. I'm too hot.
   d Sorry to bother you, but there's no tea or coffee in my room.

3 *Your own answers. Possible answers*:
   a Sorry to bother you, but there's no hot water in my bathroom.
   b Sorry, but I asked for a room with a bath and there is only a shower in this room.
   c I'm afraid that the television doesn't work.
   d Sorry, but the bathroom is dirty and the toilet won't flush.
   e Sorry, but I ordered a meal from room service an hour ago and I'm still waiting.

Unit 9

Get ready to listen and speak...

○ *Your own answers.*

○ a 7   b 2   c 5   d 3   e 4   f 6   g 8   h 1

A

1 b How long does it take?
   c What time's the next train?
   d Which platform does it leave from?

3 b How much is it?
   c How long does it take?
   d What time's the next train?
   e Which platform does it leave from?

B

1 a Edinburgh: 7.45, Platform 1   b York: 7.49, Platform 3
   c Cambridge: 8.15, Platform 9   d Liverpool: 8.10, Platform 7

2 e 2   f 4   g 6   h 3   i 1   j 5

3 b 10.00am   c 11.45am   d 1.00pm   e 2.30pm–4.00pm
   f 5.15pm

Focus on understanding the time

2 2 e   3 a   4 c   5 g   6 d   7 b   8 f

Answer key

C

1 a turn right

  b You turn left and go past the bank. The subway's on the left.

2 d Tourist Information Office

  e Cinema

  f Modern Art Museum

Focus on giving directions

b Turn c past d on e far f miss

Sound smart

3

  a On the right? c On Park Lane? e At four thirty?

  b On the corner? d On the left? f At nine forty-five?

D

1 Excuse me. I'm lost. How do I get to the Art Museum?
Can you tell me where the Beach Hotel is, please?

2 b How do I get to the city centre?

  c Where's the Tourist Information Office, please?

  d Can you tell me where the hospital is, please?

3 *Your own answers. Possible answers*:

  b Excuse me. How do I get to the train station?

  c Where's the internet café, please?

  d Can you tell me where the nearest supermarket is, please?

  e Excuse me. Where's the Tourist Information Office?

4 *Your own answers. Possible answers*:

  b You turn right into Broadway. You go along Broadway until you get to Hazel Street. Turn right into Hazel Street, then left into Bay Way. Then turn left again into Old Roman Way.

  c You go along Station Road and turn right into Nether Street. Turn left into Oak Street and then turn right into Westway. Henry's Wine Bar is on the right.

  d Yes. It's on the High Street. Go along Station Road and turn right into Market Street. Then turn left into Merton Street. That joins the High Street. Turn right onto the High Street. The supermarket is on the left, at the end of the High Street.

  e From Station Road, you turn right into Broadway. Go along Broadway, then turn right into North Passage. You'll see the Tourist Information Office on the left.

Unit 10

Get ready to listen and speak

◐ b 3 c 6 d 5 e 4 f 1

◐ *Your own answers.*

◐ b 3 c 4 d 1 e 2

A

1 b museums c go shopping d temples

  e guided tour

2 2 a 3 e 4 c 5 b

Focus on there is/there are

b There's a c Are there any d There are e Is there a

f There are g Are there any h There's a

B

1 They mention: the Statue of Liberty, the Metropolitan Museum of Art, Central Park, Times Square

2 They decide to go to the Statue of Liberty, Central Park, and Times Square.

C

1 How about going to the Metropolitan Museum of Art?
What about going to Central Park?
Let's go there first.

2 1 c 2 b 3 a

3 Jim and Denise say: *I'd rather not do that today.   That's a good idea.   That sounds great.   That's fine with me.*

4 *Your own answers. Possible answers*:

  b Let's go to the Guggenheim Museum.

  c What about seeing the Empire State Building?

  d Let's go to the Metropolitan Museum of Art.

  e How about looking round Central Park?

  f Why don't we go to Times Square?

D

1 1 The Rocks 2 Sydney Opera House 3 the Botanic Gardens 4 Darling Harbour 5 the Aquarium

2 a 1 b 4 c 2 d 3 e 5

3 Bill and Julie say: *How amazing!   How beautiful!   It's fantastic!   It's huge!*

Focus on adjectives

beautiful–ugly cheap–expensive quiet–crowded
relaxing–stressful clean–dirty safe–dangerous
lively–boring

2 Positive: wonderful fantastic marvellous great amazing
Negative: terrible awful disappointing dreadful disgusting

E

1 The bus takes route C.

2 b False (He designed the building, and everything inside.)

  c False (It was built as an apartment block and office building.)

  d False (It was built between 1905 and 1910.)

  e True

  f True (It is still unfinished.)

F

2 *Your own answers. Possible answers*:

  b The people are wonderful. They're very friendly.

  c The night life is great. It's very lively.

  d It's quite expensive.

  e The hotel is a bit disappointing. It's quite dirty.

  f There's a lot to see. It's a very interesting place.

  g The beach is fantastic. It's very clean.

3 *Your own answers. Possible answers*:
Rome is really beautiful. The people are very friendly and there's a lot to see. The buildings are very old. The food is wonderful, and it's quite cheap. It's quite crowded and a little bit dirty, but it's a very interesting place. I love it!

Review 1

Section 1
1 a **2** b **3** c **4** b **5** a **6** c **7** a **8** c **9** a **10** a

Section 2
1 a **2** c **3** b **4** b **5** a **6** b **7** c **8** a **9** b **10** b

Section 3
1 b **2** a **3** a **4** a **5** b **6** c **7** a **8** b **9** c **10** c

Section 4
Your own answers. Possible answers:

1 That's a good idea. / That sounds great. / I'd rather not do that today. / I don't really want to do that.
2 OK. I'll pay by credit card.
3 I'll have steak, please. / I'll have the chicken, please.
4 It was fine, thanks. / It was great. / It was busy/boring.
5 Oh dear. Poor you! / I hope you feel better soon. / I'm sorry to hear that. How awful. / Perhaps you should see a doctor.
6 Yes, that's right. / That's correct.
7 Go along here and turn right/left. It's on the corner/opposite the train station.
8 How amazing! It's huge! It's fantastic! It's wonderful!
9 Oh really? Why's that? / Have you got any plans? / Are you doing anything special?
10 I'm here on business / holiday.

Unit 11

Get ready to listen and speak

○ *Your own answers. Possible answers:*
The man might be saying *Do you have a brochure? Have you got details?*
The woman might be saying *Here's a brochure. / Have you seen our brochure?*
The man might be saying *I've got a meeting with … Where do I go?*
The woman might be saying *Follow me. Please come this way.*
The man might be saying *How much is it? What features does it have?*
The woman might be saying *This is a popular model. / It's on special offer.*

A

1 a 2 b 1 c 3
2 a ✓ b ✓ c ✗ d ✓
3 b I'll c Shall I

B

1 I'll give you a hand.
Shall I help you?
2 *Your own answers. Possible answers:*
b Don't worry. Let me find another one for you.
c Yes, of course. It's over there. Shall I show you the way?
d That's OK. I'll get another one for you.
e Let me help you. Shall I take it to your car?

C

1 b Meeting Room 4 c sales report d meeting at two o'clock
e the key
2 2 b 3 e 4 a 5 c

3 b Chris – bring this week's business report to John's office.
c Helen – take store key to reception.
d Lisa – meeting in Room 2 at three o'clock.
e George – report is for Jan 3rd not 8th.

D

2 *Your own answers. Possible answers:*
b George wants you to send the sales figures to him.
c Mikael in the sales department wants you to phone him. He said it's urgent.
d Mr Lee wants you to meet him in the conference room at two o'clock. He said it's important.
e The production manager wants you to prepare a report for her.

E

1 a send an email to Helen. Tell her there's a meeting next Tuesday …
b call David Green. Ask him to send the report
c ask Bob if he can come at five
d email John at head office. Ask him to come to next week's presentation.
e make six copies of the Clarkson file by lunchtime
2 b ✗ c ✓ d ✗ e ✓

F

1 a Thanks very much for coming.
b Well, I hope to see you again soon. Have a safe journey.
2 *Your own answers. Possible answers:*
d OK. It was great to see you again. Thanks very much for coming.
e OK. I hope to see you again soon. Have a safe journey.
f Yes. Thanks very much for coming.

Unit 12

Get ready to listen and speak

○ *Your own answers.*

A

1 The callers mention: desks, photocopiers, printer cartridges, envelopes, and computers.
2 The company does not sell photocopiers or computers.
3 b discount c charge d special e deliver
4 2 e 3 d 4 a 5 b

Focus on some/any

b some c some d any e some

B

1 Can you find out the price, please?
Could you call me when the order is ready?
2 5 No, that's everything. Can you deliver?
2 Yes, we do. We sell all sizes of paper.
6 Yes, we deliver free of charge.
3 I'd like to order three boxes of A3, please.
1 Hello. Do you sell A3 paper?
4 Certainly. Three boxes. Anything else?

Answer key

4 *Your own answers. Possible answers*:
b   Do you sell computers? Can you give me a discount?
c   Do you charge for delivery? Could you deliver on Tuesday?
d   Do you have any large envelopes? Can you send my order special delivery?
e   Do you sell desks? Could you find out the price for me?

5 *Your own answers. Possible answers*:
b   Hello. Can you give me some information about your prices, please?
c   Hello. Can you come early today please? The office is very dirty.
d   Could you book a room for Mr Matsumoto? He's coming tonight. Thanks a lot.
e   Hello. We need some office furniture urgently. When can you deliver?

C

1 b   Positive   c   Negative   d   Positive
2 b   4   c   3   d   1   e   2
4 *Your own answers. Possible answers*:
g   No, I'm afraid not. That's our best price.
h   Sure. No problem. But it'll cost €12 extra.
i   Sorry, I'm afraid I can't. I can repair it tomorrow though.
j   Yes, that's fine. I'll keep it until 5pm.

D

large desk   Quantity: 2   Catalogue no.: 3743   Price: £175
Executive chair   Quantity: 1   Catalogue no.: 984a   Price: £78
Total: 502.90 (incl. VAT)

Focus on adjectives

1 b   small   c   expensive   d   inefficient   e   badly-made
2 large–larger–largest   cheap–cheaper–cheapest
easy–easier–easiest   reliable–more reliable–most reliable
efficient–more efficient–most efficient
difficult–more difficult–most difficult

E

1 Emily buys the T150 (the bigger printer, on the left).
2 T150: Advantage: cheaper   Disadvantage: very big
X80: Advantage: quicker   Disadvantage: the wrong colour
3 Emily says: *I think I'll get* the T150.

F

2 *Your own answers. Possible answers*:
The TriStar is more expensive than the Maxi. The screen is also smaller.
The Maxi's got a bigger screen than the TriStar, but the TriStar has more memory. The Maxi is quicker.

Unit 13

Get ready to listen and speak
○ *Your own answers.*
◐ *Your own answers.*

A

1 David c, Kevin a, Charles b
2 a   Paul is the receptionist.   b   tomorrow.
c   He's out of the office.   d   He's on another call.
e   She asks him to call her when he's free.

Focus on telephoning

2 b   calling   c   leave   d   hold   e   speak   f   put
g   busy   h   call

B

1 b   I'm afraid I didn't quite catch that.
c   Sorry. How do you spell that?
d   Can you speak a bit more slowly, please?
2 2   d   3   b   4   a
3 *Your own answers. Possible answers*:
b   I'm afraid I didn't quite catch that. / Sorry. Can you repeat that, please?
c   Can you speak a bit more slowly, please?
d   Sorry. How do you spell that?
e   I'm afraid I didn't quite catch that. / Sorry. Can you repeat that, please?

Sound smart

2 /ei/ a, j, k, h   /iː/ b, c, d, e, g, p, t, v   /e/ f, l, m, n, s, x, z
/ai/ i, y   /əu/ o   /uː/ q, u, w   /aː/ r
3 b   Sophia   c   Jonathon   d   Thomson   e   Mary Anne

C

1 a   2   b   3   c   1
2 David Brown
wants to meet on Friday at 12.45 pm
Call 0207-9845-6109
Susan from Accounts
can't find my sales report (needs it before 4pm)
Call asap. Extension 790
Robert Macintyre from Shell International
Office: 0190-456-0280 (before 3.15 pm)
Mobile: 07967-7635423 (after 6.30 pm)

Sound smart

2 d   212-691-4078   e   0161-310-4639
f   01482-886-291   g   810-5390-2681

D

1 2   b, h   3   f, j   4   d, g   5   c, i
2 *Your own answers. Possible answers*:
b   Hi. This is … . I'm phoning because we need to arrange a meeting. Please ring me back. My number is 0465-013-645. Talk to you later. Bye for now.

c Hello. My name is … . I'm phoning to ask about your prices. Could you send me a brochure, please? My address is 45 Green Street, Manchester, MN1 6TR. Thank you. Goodbye.

d Hello. It's … . I'm calling to tell you that I've finished the report. Please ring me back on my cell phone. The number is 07960 235648. Thanks a lot. Bye.

Unit 14

Get ready to listen and speak

○ *Your own answers.*
○ *Your own answers.*
○ 1 Welcome 2 Introduction 3 Main section
   4 Conclusion 5 Questions and answers

A

1 George 2, Amy 3, Ben 1
2 b marketing strategy (for this year)
   c new ordering system
3 b presentation
   c talk

B

1 3 show you how to order.
   1 talk about the new computer program.
   4 tell you how to contact us.
   2 explain how to search for a product.
2 The signposts Mike uses are: *To start with / Then / After that / Finally*

Sound smart

2 After <u>that</u> I'll <u>show</u> you how to <u>order</u>, and <u>finally</u> I'll <u>tell</u> you how to <u>contact</u> us if you <u>have</u> a <u>problem</u>.

C

1 a First b Second c Third d lastly
2 a address b product / order c quantity d sales number

D

1 b False (when the system is ready, it will save …)
   c False (there won't be so many mistakes)
   d True (it should save us money)
2 In conclusion … Thanks for coming.
3 To sum up … Thank you very much for listening.

E

1 b Agrees c Disagrees d Agrees e Disagrees f Agrees
2 b good point c don't think d agree e wrong
   f right.

Focus on giving opinions

☹ a bit boring / not that good
☺ OK / all right
☺ really good / very interesting

F

1 b 1 c 1 d 2 e 2
2 4 Oh dear. Why do you think that?
   2 I liked it. I think it was very interesting.
   1 What did you think of the presentation?
   3 Really? I don't agree. I think it was a bit boring.
   5 Because there was nothing new in it.
4 *You own answers. Possible answers:*
   b I think it was OK. c Yes, it was really good.
   d I didn't enjoy it very much.
   e Yes, it was very interesting. f Yes, I agree. It was a bit boring.

Unit 15

Get ready to listen and speak

○ *Your own answers.*
○ *Your own answers.*

A

1 The topic of the seminar is education.
2 a True b False (it stands for *Education for All*)
   c True d True e False (there are around 20 million more)

B

2 In the seminar we hear: *Can you say a bit more about that, please?*
3 *Your own answers. Possible answers:*
   b Could you go into more detail on that, please?
   c Can you explain that, please?
   d What do you mean exactly?
   e Can you say a bit more about that, please?

C

1 Sam: b, e Teresa: d Kate: a, c
2 I agree.
   I don't agree.
   I'm not sure I agree.

D

1 a I agree completely. b I don't agree at all.
2 b 1 c 3 d 5 e 6 f 2
3 *Your own answers. Possible answers:*
   b No, I don't agree. c Yes, I agree completely.
   d No, I'm not sure I agree. e Yes, I think you're right.
   f No. I don't agree at all.
4 *Your own answers.*

E

1 a 1 b 2 c 1 d 2
2 *Your own answers. Possible answers:*
   b Do you agree that education should be free to everyone?
   c Do you think children have the right to a good education?
   d Do you think that children should learn about politics at school?
   e Do you agree that schools should teach religion?
   f Do you think poor families should get money to send their children to school?

Answer key

3   *Your own answers. Possible answers*:
   b   Yes, I think it should. / No, I think people should pay.
   c   Yes, in my opinion everyone has the right to a good education. / No, I don't agree.
   d   Yes, I think they should. / No, in my opinion they shouldn't.
   e   Yes, I think schools should teach religion. / No, in my opinion they shouldn't.
   f   Yes, in my opinion they should. / No, in my opinion they shouldn't.

F

1   a mind   b something   c point
2   a wait a minute   b ahead.   c course
3   b

Focus on Me too/Me neither

1   Me too.   Me neither.
2   a   After a positive sentence, you use *Me too.*
   b   After a negative sentence, you use *Me neither.*
3   b Me too.   c Me neither.   d Me too.   e Me too.
   f Me neither.   g Me too.   h Me neither.

Unit 16

Get ready to listen and speak

○   *Your own answers.*
○   *Your own answers.*

A

1   Monika is taking five classes this term.
2   Culture Studies / 8.30am / Tuesdays and Thursdays
   Social Change / 10am / Tuesdays and Thursdays
   Language Development / 2pm / Mondays, Wednesdays and Fridays
   Education / 9.40am / Mondays
   Communication Studies / 10am / Wednesdays and Fridays

Focus on prepositions

b on   c at / in   d at   e at   f on   g in   h at   i in

B

1   b   Which room is it in?
   c   How many classes are there a week?
   d   When are the classes?
   e   Who's teaching the course?
2   *Your own answers. Possible answers*:
   b   How many classes are there a week?
   c   When are the classes?
   d   Which room are they in?
   e   Who's teaching the course?
3   *Your own answers. Possible answers*:
   The course starts on Monday the fourth of September. I've got five classes a week. They're on Monday to Friday, from nine till twelve. They're in room 2A, and Mr Price is teaching the course.

C

1   Dr Grimshaw / Study Skills / 12th / Room 173
   Mr Collins / Life and Culture in the UK / 23rd / Lecture Hall
   Prof Kaminski / The Future of Computer Languages / 26th / Theatre
2   b   Everyone should go to Mr Collins' lecture.
   c   Computer Science students should go to Prof Kaminski's lecture.

D

1   b   Language and Culture
   c   Language Development   d The Future of the English Language   e How to be a successful language learner
2   b   2000 word   c five   d presentation   e one-minute
3   b   Monday morning   c Wednesday 17th   d Monday 21st
   e   next Friday

E

b   He's been ill   c today   d next Friday (the 27th)

Sound smart

2   You should make sure your voice goes up at the end of each phrase.
   a   By Wednesday?   b By Friday 3rd?
   c   By the end of next week?   d On Monday 17th?
   e   Before lunchtime tomorrow?

F

1   Mike says *I'm sorry, but …* to apologize.
3   2   Yes, what is it?
   5   Would Friday be OK?
   1   Excuse me. Mr. Gaffrey?
   3   I'm very sorry but I haven't done the report yet.
   6   Yes, that's all right. But no later than Friday, please.
   4   I see. So when can you hand it in?
4   *Your own answers. Possible answers*:
   b   I'm really sorry, but I haven't done my project. Can I give it to you next Friday?
   c   I'm afraid I haven't done my homework. Would tomorrow be OK?
   d   I'm sorry, but I haven't finished my English project. Could I hand it in next week?
   e   I'm afraid I haven't quite finished my course work. Can I give it to you tomorrow?

Focus on asking for permission

1   b
2   b   Would Monday be OK?
   c   Can I give my homework to you tomorrow?
   d   Could I hand in my project next week?

Review 2

Section 1
1 c   2 c   3 b   4 a   5 a   6 c   7 b   8 c   9 b   10 b
Section 2
1 b   2 b   3 a   4 c   5 c   6 a   7 a   8 c   9 c   10 b
Section 3
1 a   2 b   3 b   4 c   5 a   6 b   7 b   8 a   9 a   10 b

<u>Section 4</u>

Possible answers:

1 Sorry, that's the best price we can offer you. / Yes, we can give an extra 5% off.
2 OK, but only until then. / Yes, no problem.
3 Yes, thanks. That's very kind of you. / No thanks. I'm all right.
4 Yes, we deliver free of charge. / No, I'm sorry we can't. / Yes, we can deliver but we charge £10.
5 I'll give you a hand. / Let me help you. / Shall I help you?
6 It was a bit boring. / It was great.
7 Me too. / Really? I thought it was useful.
8 Sure, go ahead. / Yes, that's OK. / Can you wait while I finish? / Can I finish what I'm saying first?
9 Oh really? Why not? / I thought it was OK. / Me neither.
10 Yes, I'll try. / I think so. / I'm not sure. / No, I'm afraid not. Would next Monday be OK?

CAMBRIDGE

English Language Teaching

Real skills for real life

A brand new, four-level skills series

For photocopiable skills activities, try these Copy Collection titles...

Book & Audio CD
978-0-521-60848-0

Book
978-0-521-53287-7

Book
978-0-521-53405-5

Book
978-0-521-60582-3

Book & Audio CDs (2)
978-0-521-75461-3

Book & Audio CD
978-0-521-75464-4

Book
978-0-521-55981-2
Cassette
978-0-521-55980-5

Book
978-0-521-55979-9
Cassette
978-0-521-55978-2

Book
978-0-521-62612-5
Cassettes
978-0-521-62611-8

Please order through your usual bookseller.
In case of difficulty, please contact:

**ELT Marketing, Cambridge University Press,
The Edinburgh Building,
Cambridge, CB2 8RU, UK**

**Tel: +44 (0)1223 325922
Fax: +44 (0)1223 325984**

Listening & Speaking

Level 1

With answers &
Audio CDs (2)
978-0-521-70198-3
Without answers
978-0-521-70199-0

Level 2

With answers &
Audio CDs (2)
978-0-521-70200-3
Without answers
978-0-521-70201-0

Level 3

With answers &
Audio CDs (2)
978-0-521-70588-2
Without answers
978-0-521-70589-9

Level 4

With answers &
Audio CDs (2)
978-0-521-70590-5
Without answers
978-0-521-70591-2

Writing

Level 1

With answers & Audio CD
978-0-521-70184-6
Without answers
978-0-521-70185-3

Level 2

With answers & Audio CD
978-0-521-70186-0
Without answers
978-0-521-70187-7

Level 3

With answers & Audio CD
978-0-521-70592-9
Without answers
978-0-521-70593-6

Level 4

With answers & Audio CD
978-0-521-70594-3
Without answers
978-0-521-70595-0

Reading

Level 1

With answers
978-0-521-70202-7
Without answers
978-0-521-70203-4

Level 2

With answers
978-0-521-70204-1
Without answers
978-0-521-70205-8

Level 3

With answers
978-0-521-70573-8
Without answers
978-0-521-70574-5

Level 4

With answers
978-0-521-70575-2
Without answers
978-0-521-70576-9

Bring your skills to life

For teacher's notes, visit: **www.cambridge.org/englishskills**